STUDYING FOR A DEGREE

RELATED TITLES FROM MACMILLAN

How to Study: A Practical Guide   *Frank Casey*

Mastering Study Skills   *R. Freeman*

Learning History: A Guide to Advanced Study   *Richard Brown
and Christopher Daniels*

STUDYING FOR A DEGREE

in the Humanities and Social Sciences

Patrick Dunleavy

MACMILLAN

First published 1986 by
MACMILLAN EDUCATION LTD
Houndmills, Basingstoke, Hampshire RG21 2XS
and London
Companies and representatives
throughout the world

ISBN 0–333–41842–5

A catalogue record for this book is available
from the British Library

Printed in Hong Kong

5th Reprint 1992

Contents

Preface

Universities, polytechnics and colleges still devote negligible resources to formalized teaching of study skills compared with those they expend on conveying to students the substantive ideas of degree subjects. Fifteen years of discontent with this situation, first as a student and subsequently as a teacher, underlie my decision to write this book. No doubt a large number of my colleagues will distrust the whole enterprise, as yet another stage on the slippery slope of 'spoonfeeding' students. I hope none the less that the book will be useful for students and teachers concerned with advising them.

My approach is distinctive in three ways. First, I have aimed solely to offer suggestions suitable for students on degree courses in the humanities and social sciences. There are many books in print designed for lower level courses, most of which are quite useful in their way but are not appropriate for students at degree level. Second, I distrust some study skills books because of their puritanical tone and tendency to fuss over trivial details, while neglecting more fundamental intellectual problems. I have tried neither to insult my readers' intelligence by dealing with obvious or minor incidentals, nor to legislate unrealistic levels of work input or radical personality changes as prerequisites for improvements in studying. Third, I am acutely aware that reading a single book of this kind cannot in itself change anyone's study methods for the better. My role is simply to offer suggestions which people who already want to improve their approaches to studying may find useful as models to try out for themselves. Although I have set out my ideas as coherently and persuasively as possible, I have no expectation that more than a fraction of them will be useful to or be adopted by any reader. None the less I hope that by appraising their own study methods against these suggestions, readers will be able to review their own methods of working in a self-critical and reasonably systematic way, strengthening their own approach in some areas and experimenting elsewhere with some of the ideas set out here.

I have accumulated far more intellectual debts during the

book's gestation than any set of acknowledgments could reasonably list. Mary Geffen, Judith Riley, Andy Blowers, Chris Hamnett and others on the Open University's D202 Course Team in 1978–82 were critically supportive. A short course at the University Teaching Methods Unit in London stimulated further thinking. Euan Henderson of IET and the Institute of Education library in London filled in vital gaps in my reading. At the LSE George Jones, Brendan O'Leary, and many others influenced my thinking in lots of ways I hope they will recognize. My wife Sheila and my father Vincent between them hammered the ideas and the prose into better shape. Macmillan's editors Vanessa Peerless and Steven Kennedy provided the kind of committed publishing support which makes being one of their authors a real pleasure. Comments from seven anonymous readers in different disciplines produced a radical change in the final manuscript. To all these people, and the many whom space prohibits me from listing, go my sincere thanks. Finally my greatest debt is owed to all my students at the LSE, the Open University and Oxford, who have sifted my advice with unfailing tolerance over the years, and stimulated any useful suggestions in these pages.

LSE   PATRICK DUNLEAVY
February 1986

Comments on any aspect of the book and suggestions for future editions would be very welcome: write to me at LSE, Houghton Street, London WC2A 2AE.

Acknowledgements

The author and publishers wish to thank the following, who have kindly given permission for the use of copyright material:

Professors B. N. Lewis and D. C. Hawkridge for quotations from an unpublished 1974 report by the Open University Institute of Education to the Ford Foundation on 'New Methods of Assessment and Stronger Methods of Curriculum Design', written by B. N. Lewis in collaboration with C. Byrne, D. Hawkridge, M. Neil, G. Paske and D. Roberts.

Routledge and Kegan Paul for figure 3.4 from H. J. Eysenck, 'Primary Social Attitudes', *British Journal of Sociology* (1951) p. 198.

How to Read this Book

There are seven chapters in the book, arranged in a sequence which roughly mirrors a student's progress through college. The first chapter deals with 'Starting off in higher education' and is intended mainly for people who are just about to go to university/college or who are in their first year there. If you are an experienced student, you may still find it useful to read this chapter fairly quickly.

The next three chapters tackle different aspects of normal coursework. Chapter 2 deals with 'Generating information', finding literature, using it effectively, and making notes. Chapter 3 describes 'Analysing concepts and theories', particularly explaining how to place problem concepts within a whole field of ideas. Once you have gathered enough information and you understand the major concepts involved in an area, Chapter 4 moves on to 'Writing essays'. It describes how to de-bug essay topics, plan your response, and write up finished text.

The next two chapters relate to course assessment. You may move on in your final year to 'Writing dissertations', the subject of Chapter 5. Dissertations pose some problems over and above ordinary essay writing, especially in organizing research, writing up a longer piece of text and referencing sources. Chapter 6 deals with the final and most critical stage in most courses, 'Revising for exams' and answering exam questions.

Chapter 7 on 'Turning study skills into life skills' is likely to be of immediate relevance if you are beginning the 'milk round' of career interviews and job applications. However, it is worth reading well in advance of this stage, since by then it is generally rather late to do anything about acquiring career-relevant skills. The earlier you think through some ideas about possible career lines, the greater the opportunity you have to undertake relevant activities and develop key personal qualities.

Although the whole book can quite sensibly be tackled in the sequence set out here, it can also be read and re-read in smaller sections, as and when you need to find out about something.

Each chapter is designed to be read easily and some additional study aids are included for this purpose:

A reading guide is given at the front of each chapter which describes the contents of each subsection, and gives advice about which parts might be skimmed by some readers and which need to be read carefully.

A summary of suggestions is given at the end of each chapter, listing the *practical* suggestions made for improving your study methods together with the page reference where the suggestion is explained.

The index and **the contents page** are quite detailed, and should help you to track down information on particular topics.

1 Starting Off in Higher Education

Reading Guide

Beginning your studies at degree level is a time to appreciate some fundamental aspects of working in higher education. I examine:

1. The importance of 'internalizing' knowledge – making other people's ideas and expertise your own.
2. Four key study activities – writing essays, attending classes, individual tutorials, and lectures.
3. How to get better at studying as you progress in your courses.

Experienced students may wish to skim section 1.2, but should find some new ideas and suggestions in section 1.3.

1.1 MAKING KNOWLEDGE YOUR OWN

Students in higher education are expected to master some fairly esoteric materials. Most people find it hard to learn complex, abstract and unfamiliar matter, but easier to understand information if it relates directly to their own needs and experiences. For example, if you had never been to London and were asked to memorize a map of the 'Tube', the underground railway system, you would probably find it fairly difficult. These maps present a dense mass of information about dozens of stations and multiple Tube lines in a highly stylized form. In practice, however, almost nobody tries to memorize the whole system. Instead people learn the principles of the underground map, because they use bits of it frequently. They discover immediately if they make mistakes (by ending up in the wrong station), and the Tube map connects easily with a great deal of other knowledge that they already have – about places, neighbourhoods, and more conventional street maps. Above all, the Tube map meets a pressing practical need – how to get from one point to another – which provides a strong motivation to learn how to use it. This motivation is reinforced by rewards. You get quicker and more flexible access to a wide variety of locations when you understand how the underground system works.

The knowledge taught in higher education is often very specialized and abstract. It usually cannot be used in precisely the form in which it is learnt except on a university or polytechnic course. Most humanities and social science degrees are non-vocational, so students may not re-employ much of their course knowledge in their later careers. Making mistakes in interpreting new information rarely produces direct effects. The most concentrated feedback from exams or assessment comes at the end of a course, when the opportunities for further learning are minimal. Finally maintaining the motivation to go on with academic study can be a problem. Many pay-offs from academic work (such as 'intellectual development') are diffuse and long-term benefits. They can easily seem important only within the context of higher education itself.

Consequently a central problem in higher education is how to internalize academic knowledge – that is, connect up the new material with things that we already know, and understand how to use it for our own purposes. To make knowledge our own we must convert it from being 'other people's knowledge' to being part of our own ways of thinking. Achieving this kind of depth learning is the central problem with which study activities in college are designed to cope. During the lengthy evolution of higher education, four key study activities have been developed in the humanities and social sciences to encourage students to internalize knowledge. Writing essays, going to classes and seminars, having individual tutorials, and listening to lectures are all long-established features of higher education systems. They are almost as important now as they were a hundred years ago. These core activities have increasingly been supplemented by new methods – such as project work and programmed learning. But the enduring importance of traditional learning methods reflects their high level of effectiveness in helping students to incorporate academic knowledge into their own ways of thinking.

1.2 FOUR KEY STUDY ACTIVITIES

Essay Writing

The central focus of degree work in the humanities and the non-technical social sciences is on students' producing regular essays or papers which summarize and express their personal understanding of a topic. Writing essays forces you to select what you find plausible or interesting in books and journals, and to express your understanding in a coherent form. You have to consider different views and perspectives, and achieve some level of personal synthesis. Individual written work also provides teachers with the best available guide to how you are progressing in a subject, and allows them to give advice on how to develop your strengths or counteract your weaknesses. Lastly, of course, individual written work is still the basis of almost all assessment in higher education. Written assignments familiarize you with the form that your exams or coursework papers will take.

The order of emphasis here is internalizing knowledge first, intellectual development second, generating feedback third, and practising for assessment fourth. Yet many people reverse these priorities, viewing essay writing chiefly as a test of how they will do in exams. This attitude is extremely restrictive. It ignores the importance of cumulative intellectual development during a course, the value of written work in forcing you to make choices amongst materials and viewpoints, and the constructive impact of teachers' comments in suggesting new ways forward.

Writing essays is a time-consuming business and each assignment gives you intensive knowledge only about one particular topic, rather than a wider sense of a whole course. But four or five essays will begin to show cumulative effects and linkages. So in each of your subjects you need to envisage a programme of written work to build up your knowledge over the lifetime of the course. In the humanities and social sciences the norm is to write around one essay or assignment every two weeks or ten days, although the emphasis on written work at different institutions may be less. In deciding how much written work you need to do, a simple minimum test asks: Will you have written as many essays during a course as are required in the end-of-year examination? If not, you are writing too little.

Essay writing is such a key study task that the whole of Chapter 4 is devoted to discussing it in detail. For the moment we need only note its central features to see how it differs from and fits in with other activities.

Seminars and Class Discussions

Seminars and class discussions help you to internalize academic knowledge by providing specialized contexts in which to talk about such esoteric problems as the trade-off between inflation and unemployment in economic policy, or the use of metaphors in Shakespeare's drama.

> Talking is a basic human art. By it each communicates to others what he knows and, at the same time, provokes the contradictions which direct his attention to what he has overlooked.

> (Lonergan, 1958, p. 174)

Talking is a more fragmented and more interactive activity than written work. In a conversation you can keep tabs on how effectively you are expressing a viewpoint, and modify what you are saying in response to people's reactions. In addition a normal programme of between ten and twenty-five classes will cover far more topics in one subject than you can hope to manage in your written work. Participating in flexible conversations across this range of issues allows you to practise using the broader knowledge gained from lectures and background reading, and helps you select topics where you want to complete written assignments. Even sitting in a class and confining your involvement to 'active listening' can be valuable in recalling material to your attention. You have to run through your own understanding, assess other people's views, and pinpoint areas where there is disagreement. You can seek a directly personalized explanation of problems which no lecture or textbook can provide. And the presence of the class teacher should ensure that sources of confusion are clarified and the group's discussions are checked for accuracy.

Some modern philosophers argue that human communication is premissed upon a fundamental assumption of equality between the participants. Misunderstandings and misconstructions arise principally from differences in status or power between participants in communication (Habermas, 1971). Whether or not you find such views plausible, they do capture one of the fundamental dilemmas of seminars. Group discussions and classes are most useful as conversational forums where they permit flexible, multi-way discussion. Unlike tutorials, the role of the teacher need not be obtrusively dominant. Teachers can assume a 'facilitating' rather than a 'directing' role, getting individual students to start off each week's discussion with a prepared oral presentation, possibly accompanied by a photocopied paper. If class participation is to be widespread then some individuals will need to refrain from talking too much while others have to be persuaded to break their customary silence. Similarly student members of classes need to have some prior acquaintance with the week's topic and be prepared to think 'on their feet' if the class is to be valuable.

These conditions are not often realized in all aspects. In some subjects teachers view classes as much more directly instructional, a sort of small-group lecture where the teacher talks most of the time, and student interaction is confined to interrupting when they cannot follow a point. This style may be appropriate in very technical subjects, such as formal logic, linguistics, statistics or aspects of economics. Nonetheless there are more interactive ways of teaching such material. For example, question-and-answer methods are a more effective way to get class members to work through an apparatus of technical concepts for themselves, rather than listening to their class teacher simply reiterating the main lecture points. Unlike 'conversational' classes, 'instructional' classes have much less interaction amongst class members. Their patterns of communication sometimes resemble those psychological experiments where people in a partitioned room can pass messages only via an intermediary (the teacher) occupying a central section.

Students themselves may frustrate the potential for fruitful conversation – for example, by refusing to prepare effective oral presentations from notes, instead reading out a complete essay; or giving only sketchy comments which provide no basis for further discussion. Class members may sit passively, refusing to contribute unless asked, and directing questions or comments not to each other but to the teacher who 'knows the answers'. If classes are marked by long silences or halting discussion, students frequently blame the teacher rather than themselves. But like any other conversation, small group discussions are only as good as all the participants make them. Just as a monologue by one person cannot revive a flagging conversation, so teachers can only puncture class silences by asserting a dominance which pushes the class automatically into a more didactic, instructional format.

So if your classes are not working because your class teacher talks all the time, no one else joins in discussions, or the same people do all the talking, it is still important that you persevere. Have you done anything to try and alter things, for example, by interrupting the teacher's flow of words with more questions or by playing your own part more fully? If you find the discussions going over your head, are you turning up 'cold' to the class sessions, expecting to get all the cues you need for discussion from the oral presentation, or perhaps expecting just to make notes on what the class teacher has to say? If you find it hard to participate, have you worked out a few questions that bother you to ask in one of the gaps in the discussions?

Individual Tutorials

Discussions between a teacher and one or two students are used in many colleges as a substitute for, or a supplement to, group discussions in classes. Tutorials can range from direct expositions by the teacher in technical subjects, to flexible conversational sessions which at their best are very effective in stimulating mastery of a body of knowledge. The one-to-one quality of the personal interaction is very important in stimulating acceptance of ideas and producing fruitful interaction. In theory students should be much more able to control the pace and flow of material being covered to fit in with their individual needs, a big advantage over classes, especially in more technical subjects.

However, the very direct personal relationship between tutors and students can also create problems. In any dialogue people 'gloss over' points in what the other person is saying, letting material that they do not fully understand slip by in the general flow of talk, gestures and eye contact which compose the conversation. In tutorials this effect often inhibits students from frankly expressing their difficulties to their teacher. Anxiety to maintain a good impression, plus a feeling that you will be seen as a failure if you constantly interrupt to ask for clarification, can leave you nodding agreement while struggling to keep abreast of your tutor's flow of reasoning. Especially in technical subjects these personal considerations can effectively undermine the advantages of the tutorial mode. Nor can tutors easily cope with this problem. If they ask more direct questions to check up on how much of the material you are absorbing, it may only make you more nervous of 'being found out'.

If you experience these difficulties with tutorials, the most important step in combating them is to adjust your own attitudes. Most tutors like teaching and explaining things – the chief reason why they sometimes talk a lot. They will be stimulated if you ask more questions, and encouraged by the opportunity to target their explanations more specifically on the things which you find difficult. What most tutors dislike is the feeling that they are 'talking in a vacuum', with students pretending to follow even if they are actually rather confused. Often a bit more preparation for tutorials can help improve what you get out of them. For example, if you want to ask your tutor's advice on an issue, think about your difficulties in advance and maybe write down a list of the points which you need to discuss. Always make sure that you provide your tutor with enough information to give useful advice. For example, if you want to discuss what topic to tackle for a dissertation do not rely on outlining your ideas orally – get a synopsis down on paper so that your teacher can get a better idea of what you envisage doing. Similarly, if you find it difficult to make notes, don't just talk about them in the abstract: show your tutor some concrete examples of how you make notes and ask if she can see any avenues for improvement.

Of course, this advice cannot cover all situations. Not all tutors are capable of empathizing with all their students. Therefore the difficulties may well lie on their side rather than yours. In the hopefully exceptional circumstances where a personal relationship has no real chance of succeeding, most colleges and departments make provision for students to change tutors. There is usually someone on the academic staff (with a title such as 'departmental tutor', 'course tutor', or Dean) who can arrange a transfer to another teacher. Changing tutors is not always easy to do and it may cause some disruption in your work patterns. So if it is necessary, make sure that you transfer fairly early on in a year.

Lectures

Lectures play a large part in most students' timetables and occupy a considerable proportion of teachers' efforts. Yet most academic institutions do not see them as of absolutely critical significance for students' progress. Unlike classes or tutorials, lectures are usually voluntary: no one checks up to see if you go or not. In the humanities and social sciences, levels of lecture attendance vary widely across different institutions. At Oxford University, for example, most undergraduates 'shop around' several lecture courses at the start of term, but within a few weeks drop most of them. In most universities and polytechnics, however, class teaching follows the sequence of lecture topics, and lecturers set the end-of-year exams. Here the norm is for students to religiously attend lectures.

The major difficulty with lectures is that they are not interactive. The lecturer normally talks for the whole time with minimal feedback from questions. Making notes in lectures while concentrating on the argument being developed is often difficult (see pp. 43–4). Most research suggests that people can recall only about a third of a lecture's contents after one week, so unless good notes are provided or can be made during the talk the learning residue involved may not be great. Many students who make their own notes in lectures never consult them again, even during exam revision (Gibbs, 1981, p. 59).

The comparative effectiveness of lectures and classes in helping students to learn remains a fiercely disputed area of educational research, with different empirical studies reaching opposed conclusions (Bligh, 1970, Ch. 1).

However, lectures are clearly valuable in several specific ways. They can provide a useful overview – an aerial map to familiarize you with the main landscape features to be encountered during a course. Lecturers typically give much more accessible descriptions of theoretical perspectives in their oral presentations than can be found in the academic literature. Wherever there is a rapid pace of research progress, lectures are indispensable in condensing the 'oral wisdom' of a discipline several years before the new material is incorporated into student textbooks or review articles in journals. Lastly, lectures are often very useful in allowing you to see directly how exponents of different views build up their arguments. The cues provided by seeing someone talking in person may seem 'irrelevant', but they are important aids to understanding.

Other Study Activities

There are several other important study activities.

(a) **General reading** is strongly recommended in most study skills books, and you will undoubtedly have to 'read around' most of your courses to some extent. But background reading is a predominantly passive undertaking because it is not orientated to a specific question which you are tackling in an essay or class discussion. Hence it can be very unfocused. Similarly, because you have no external timetable in general reading, it can be hard to pace yourself properly or to maintain your motivation. General reading is most useful as a way of covering major texts in periods when you would be unlikely to do more concentrated or effective work. For example, during vacations background reading lets you survey new courses in advance, or reinforce knowledge from the last term's work. Similarly it can be quite effective to browse through big books piecemeal in your bathroom or during the late evening, when assimilating them would otherwise be a major chore. As a general rule, however, reading is most effective where you are searching for answers to questions, rather than scanning for information which might conceivably be useful in a future undefined study context.

(b) Some important forms of **project learning** give students direct contact with the phenomena they are studying. The personal experience gained from seeing things at first hand, completing an experiment yourself, or acting a role, can be very useful in helping you to internalize knowledge. Field trips are increasingly used in geography, archaeology, anthropology, and history. Visits, secondments and group work play a key role in social administration or communication studies. Psychology students gather a lot of experimental evidence in laboratory practicals. Simulation games are used in many otherwise literary social sciences (such as political science, international relations, or planning studies), adding a valuable albeit artificial dimension of personal experience to subjects and situations which might otherwise be treated only in abstract or second-hand terms. Drama and oral readings are vital elements in literature studies. Much project work is group-based, providing a rare opportunity for students to develop ways of working co-operatively. Students' control over group projects is often deliberately enlarged by teaching staff. Individual projects or longer research work are usually undertaken as a way of completing dissertations (see Chapter 5).

(c) The problems and high staff costs of tutorials have led some educationalists to experiment with '**programmed learning**' forms of individualized instruction, where students work through learning materials at their own pace, completing small tests before they move on to the next section. Particularly controlled by micro-computers – in the form of 'computer-assisted learning' – programmed learning packages may have a much bigger role in higher education in the near future, especially in first-year courses and more technical subjects. At present, however, this new technology remains a potential which has only just begun to be tapped.

1.3 GETTING BETTER AT STUDYING

Starting off in higher education presents you with an important opportunity to reappraise the ways in which you go about studying. Working for a degree is an important period of life-change for most students, and the intellectual advances you make in these few years often help shape your approach to a whole series of later career tasks (see Chapter 7). Accordingly, it is very important that you keep your study methods under review during this formative life-period. Do not stand still, tackling your first-year courses in the same way that you handled your schoolwork. Five steps can help to improve your approach: acquiring some general study resources; making an effort to understand your degree subject as a whole; keeping your study methods under review; clarifying your own methods of working; and developing your self-confidence.

Acquiring some General Study Resources

Your first few months in higher education normally produce a dramatic broadening of your academic horizons. Unfamiliar concepts and arguments can easily go over your head, especially if you do not know where to follow them up. Even if you conscientiously make a note of ideas or labels you do not understand, many of your normal sources, even major textbooks, will either use concepts without defining them explicitly, or refer cryptically to patterns of argument or '-isms'. To cope with these problems, some general study resources are worth acquiring, while others can be followed up in libraries. Particularly useful are the following.

(a) **A specialist 'dictionary'** for your subject. These are available cheaply in paperback in all the humanities and social science disciplines and it is a good idea to make sure you have a personal copy. Recent second-hand copies are usually quite acceptable. Appendix 1 lists the good dictionaries currently in print in each of the humanities and social science subjects. Specialist subject dictionaries generally explain not only theoretical approaches but also key concepts, the contribution of major authors and central empirical controversies.

(b) **A more general reference book to academic disciplines** such as *The Fontana Dictionary of Modern Thought* (1983) – which provides very short explanations of twentieth-century schools of thought in many different subjects – or its sister volume the *Biographical Companion* (1983). Sources such as these can be quite affordable and are particularly useful in trying to understand trans-disciplinary perspectives.

(c) **Reference works covering a number of related academic disciplines** are worth consulting in libraries. Across all the social sciences the multi-volume *International Encyclopaedia of the Social Sciences* (1968) provides authoritative essays on theories, concepts and problems in the major disciplines. All college libraries and the biggest public libraries should have a copy in their reference sections. There is no comparable source for the humanities as a group, but Appendix 1 indicates some useful comprehensive sources available in the different humanities disciplines.

Understanding your Degree Subject

Following up unfamiliar ideas or arguments will be easier and more productive if you can fit your new knowledge into a broader framework – in particular if you have some general understanding of the academic discipline you are studying. It can be hard to work out how and why your degree subject has ended up with precisely the sorts of concerns and controversies that it has. Instead of trying just to make sense of hints about the discipline's past thrown out in passing by contemporary authors, there are two types of books about your degree subject which are worth reading, perhaps especially in one of the vacations before or during your first year.

(a) **A quick history of the subject** which describes the controversies that have shaped its evolution. The most useful books are those which cover the contemporary professional development of the subject, rather than just covering major thinkers a long way back in history. Appendix 1 gives my selection of accessible short books covering each subject in the humanities and social sciences.

(b) **A 'think-book'** on the 'philosophy' or basic questions involved in your subject. These books ask from a contemporary perspective what the subject is there for, why is it worth studying, and so on. They are generally quite short and take only a couple of hours to get through. Again Appendix 1 gives a listing of suitable think-books for all the humanities and social sciences. Sometimes intellectual histories of a subject will cover this aspect as well, but often they do not.

There is a further compelling reason to make a serious effort to understand your discipline as early as you can during your period in higher education, namely the considerable risk that you may start off your studies in a subject which is not actually right for you. Picking a degree course while at school, or even when you are at college, is a difficult undertaking, since you may not have previously studied the precise area which you eventually choose. Even in a subject you are already familiar with, first-year courses are very different from schoolwork, and finals papers are much more specialized than introductory courses. Studying the wrong subject can cause a great many problems, which get worse the more time you invest in an inappropriate course. Normally, you can change your course within a broad grouping of subjects up to the beginning of your second year at college – which is one reason why you may be required to take a variety of subjects in your first year. Thereafter, you may find yourself locked-in to a course until finals.

Even if you are *basically* happy with your choice of degree, you will almost certainly be afflicted by doubts at some stage as to whether you are studying the right subject, or whether what you are studying has any real value. If you can think seriously about these issues before possibly wasting some of your precious time at university or polytechnic doing the wrong course then you can save yourself unnecessary worry or aggravation later on.

Keeping your Study Methods under Review

Since you have persevered this far, it may seem redundant advice to urge you to be self-conscious about how you study. But reading just one study skills book is only a start; by itself it is unlikely to transform your approach. Trying out new suggestions or really improving your work habits both entail quite major changes in your behaviour, which may be hard to achieve simply on your own. Therefore you should seek out opportunities to discuss your study methods with staff and fellow students.

Obviously your tutor could be the main person who helps you to improve the way you study, so long as your college has a tradition of regular teaching sessions between tutors and individual students, or allocates one member of staff to look after your academic development as a whole. But tutors tend to concentrate on getting across the substantive ideas in their subject, and for personal reasons they may not be a great help in advising on more general study methods' difficulties. There are a number of alternative sources of advice which may not occur to you but which are often helpful because they focus specifically on study methods issues.

(a) Your university or polytechnic may have a centralized **study counselling service** for dealing with students' academic work problems. Most such centres are informally run, allowing you to pop in and talk to staff, or to join small discussion groups of students.

(b) Many colleges run short **induction courses** for newly arrived first-year students on basic study methods, together perhaps with some **revision or exam preparation workshops.** These forums are well worth attending, whether they are centrally run or put on specifically for students in your subject.

Both these forms of provision can realistically help you cope only with basic study procedures – such as how to timetable work, how to read more quickly or how to make more effective notes. But because they focus your attention directly on study issues, and put you in contact with other students with similar problems, they can be very effective in getting you to change your approach.

(c) The last (and in many ways best) way to talk through study problems is by **discussion with your fellow students.** 'Peer group' learning or co-operation is well developed amongst students in North American universities, but relatively little emphasized in Britain. However, there are several areas where change is occurring. For example, women's study groups can effectively combat common problems of male dominance in class and seminar discussions. Given the frequent sex imbalance amongst lecturers and the 'gender blindness' of many academic disciplines, viewing study problems as a feminist issue can be a potent way of securing improvements in your college.

In addition to groups specifically focusing on study issues, a wide range of student societies (such as political, religious or special interest societies) often provide useful forums for discussing issues relevant to studying the humanities and social sciences. Many kinds of student discussion group can help you to translate your general values effectively into your academic work, while local groups often give personal support to members with study problems. Do not compartmentalize your life so rigidly that fruitful interconnections, and personal assistance from fellow students, are ruled out as influences on your studying.

Clarify your own Method of Working

Educational research suggests that students divide into two main groups in the ways in which they try to understand their subjects, which have been labelled 'serialists' and 'holists' (Macdonald-Ross, 1972). Serialists like to build up a network of concepts in a discipline by working piecemeal through the ideas one section at a time. These students move on from one topic or bunch of ideas to another only when it has been satisfactorily mastered. Holists (pronounced 'whole-ists'), on the other hand, like to work on several ideas or topics at once, and to look ahead quite a distance. They find that they progress better with individual topics if they have a general sense of where they are going and of the broader context of their work. Both groups of students need to understand how the ideas and topics in their courses relate to each other, but vary in the sequence in which they learn individual ideas and pull them together. Holists find that looking for an inital synthesis pays handsome dividends, while serialists focus initially on detailed ideas in the field, only subsequently pulling this knowledge together into an overall pattern. No one can say that one or other of these learning strategies is preferable for all students across all subject areas. Instead current research suggests that students have stable preferences in their style of learning and that they perform badly if their teachers or the course material try to force them to learn in a different fashion.

Many courses and textbooks are organized in a fairly uni-directional way. Traditional textbooks are characteristically serialist, requiring you to work through a predetermined sequence of topics in a linear fashion. They sometimes give few clues about the overall direction in which you are travelling. If your personal style of work is holistic, you may need to make a special effort to look ahead at the subject as a whole – for example, by reading about the basic approach of the discipline, skimming ahead to see how topics interconnect, and perhaps even looking early on at exam papers in the subject. All these activities can help you generate an advance map of the ideas in the course.

Perhaps slightly less commonly, you may encounter courses or books which start off by stressing an overall appreciation of a subject. If you work in a serialist way, then you may feel 'out of your depth' on being asked to master broad-brush features of a whole canvas before you have tackled any of the detail. Try to be relaxed if you run into problems. By skipping ahead a little to more specific topics, and leaving your own effort to achieve an overall picture to a rather later stage, you can define your own synthesis more effectively.

Developing your Self-Confidence

Many study problems ultimately involve people having too low an opinion of their own abilities or worth as an individual. If you mentally run yourself down, then it is going to be harder for you to offer your own opinions in an essay, to work co-operatively with other students, to talk to your tutor frankly, or to seize the opportunity to contribute to a class discussion. Progress in your approach to studying often depends upon, and cannot be cut off from how you are faring in other aspects of your life. Some people who become convinced that they have specific study problems (such as not being able to write essays or not participating in classes) are in fact hampered by a much more general nervousness and lack of self-confidence. If this description might apply to you, look around to see if your college offers any general groupwork or advice sessions which might be of value. 'Assertiveness training' is an especially useful forum, designed to help you to say what you really feel and to stand up for your opinions. Many women's groups offer this facility, and some students' unions lay on courses for men and women.

If you suffer from exceptionally acute anxiety about your studying, or find that you can barely do academic work at all, bear in mind the possibility that you may need more general psychological counselling. Being a student is just as stressful as any other occupation. It is a period of rapid change in your life, of separation from your parents and family, of forging new personal relationships, and of orientation towards a future in work. Teachers, courses and examinations all contribute their own specific additions to the turmoil you may be in already. Every college should provide extensive and free student health services, with doctors and counsellors who will be happy to chat with you informally about any difficulties you are experiencing. So if you are running into fundamental problems which extend beyond specific study difficulties, do not try to manage them alone. Very often just a small amount of friendly, professional advice can help you sort out problems which would otherwise prove much more painful to tackle on your own.

Summary of Suggestions: Starting off in Higher Education

1. Write at least as many essays in a subject per year as you will have to tackle in an exam (p. 6).

2. Persevere with classes which may not seem to be working – try doing some reading and thinking to prepare for classes, pinpointing questions to ask in advance, and interjecting more (p. 8).

3. Be frank about any study difficulties you may have in tutorials (p. 9).

4. Background reading is most useful when you are unlikely to do more directed study activities, for example, in vacations or during off-peak periods of the day (p. 11).

5. Do not try to approach degree work with the same study methods you used at an earlier stage in your education (p. 13).

6. Buy a specialist subject dictionary for your discipline and follow up references to concepts in related disciplines (p. 13).

7. Read a short history of your subject discipline and a book which explores its rationale either before or during your first year (p. 14).

8. Make sure you know what your subject entails, and that you will be happy working for a degree in it, early on in your period at college (p. 15).

9. Keep your study methods under review – with help from your tutor, other study counsellors, or short-term courses (p. 16).

10. Talk through study problems with other students (p. 16).

11. Be clear whether you work in a 'serialist' or a 'holist' manner. If your courses or textbooks use a different approach to a subject, take some simple steps to fit in with your style of working (p. 17).

12. Develop your own self-confidence (p. 18).

2 Generating Information

Reading Guide

Creating an information base for academic work involves:

1. Finding books and other materials.
2. 'Gutting literature' and using different kinds of sources effectively.
3. Making notes on your reading and in lectures.

Experienced students may wish to skim section 2.1, but do review it briefly since problems of accessing information can reappear later on; for example, when revising for exams.

2.1 GATHERING MATERIALS AND LITERATURE

The struggle to gain access to information sources is a *leitmotiv* of student life. Hunting for books and articles consumes a lot of time, especially in the humanities and social sciences where few courses rely on comprehensive textbooks. Normal coursework involves consulting a wide variety of separate sources tackling different aspects of a problem or expressing varying points of view. Organizing your search for information starts with the course reading lists, usually involves deciding whether to buy books, and invariably entails using one or more libraries.

Reading Lists

A 'user friendly' reading list in higher education should include:

    (i) a number of priority books and some basic course texts;
    (ii) other kinds of priority reading for the course as a whole;
    (iii) the most useful reading for each topic, organized in a

rough suggested sequence and with alternative sources
clearly indicated;

(iv) clear publication details for each entry, including a
reference number for the source in the main college
library;

(v) a specific question for each topic towards which reading
should be directed, perhaps accompanied by a brief
explanation of the issues involved.

In practice, few reading lists meet all these requirements. Poor
or inaccurate publication details are common. Introductory
reading and course texts are usually designated, but for the rest
lists are often discouragingly long and unannotated. Many
reading materials are substitutes for each other, because large
numbers of students compete at the same time for scarce library
resources. However, the overlaps in coverage from one source
to another are often not clearly indicated. As a result you can
spend a great deal of time trying to find books and articles for a
first look in order to sort out some reading priorities. Equally
you can chase up materials in case you have missed something
important, only to find that the elusive source duplicates what
you have already read. Sometimes only vague titles are used to
demarcate topics (especially in reading lists for lecture series).
This format is guaranteed to protract the search for
information, since you must guess the questions you are
supposed to be asking as well as finding out the answers. Unless
you have a specific question to respond to, you can have no
guarantee that the next item of reading might not introduce
some new question not previously encountered.

Lecturers often argue that reading lists are long and
unannotated because it is important not to bias students'
interpretation of particular sources in advance. There is
something in this point. But it is hard not to conclude that most
of the time the inaccessibility of reading lists reflects either the
lack of time teachers spend 'on compiling them, or a more
principled adherence to the 'throw 'em in the deep end' school
of thinking, for whose exponents 'spoonfeeding' students is
anathema.

When faced with a long reading list without clear priorities
or substitutes:

(a) **Buttonhole the teacher concerned** and politely insist that she indicate priorities; what would she read first if in your shoes?

(b) **Try to find modern material first**, because later literature often summarizes or criticizes earlier work. Very recent books can be a problem, however, since libraries often lag behind in their purchasing. Try your local academic bookshop for very recent books. You can always read them in the shop, even if they are not remotely affordable.

(c) **Look for literature review articles first.**

(d) **Read student-orientated books (such as textbooks) before the research literature**, since they are usually easier to understand and make reference to a broader range of materials and viewpoints.

Buying Books

Courses without textbooks and reading lists without priorities can present severe problems in deciding how many and which books you need to purchase for a course. But bear in mind that:

(a) **Primary texts** – such as major philosophical works or poems, novels and plays – are unchanging materials. So second-hand copies are perfectly acceptable, cheaper and easy to find.

(b) You will need **personal copies** of some modern books for each course if you are to read around classes or lectures. Core texts are very helpful in writing essays, and indispensable during revision for examinations. Do not buy introductory books which are unlikely to be useful throughout the course. Relying on such sources during later essay-writing or exam revision is frustrating and may cause you to undershoot the standard of argument required. If there are no whole-course textbooks, buy two or three intermediate texts (books intended for a student audience as well as for professional academics) to cover most of the topics which you are likely to tackle in essays, class papers and examinations. It is often best to defer purchasing for a few weeks so that you can work out what these books are – providing always that you will have some money left, and that copies will still be available in the bookshop.

(c) **Do not buy or order anything solely on the basis of recommendations.** Look at each book in the shop or a library. Read the blurb and any review comments on the jacket, look at the contents page and introduction, and skim the text subheadings. Check whether the book systematically reviews other literature in the area, which is almost always a plus point, or simply expounds the author's own views in a mono-thematic manner, which usually limits its usefulness. Look at the date of publication (especially when evaluating review comments on the jacket). A much republished book may be a great classic, or a lightly revised and fundamentally outdated piece of work. Check if the cover blurb identifies a market for the book. If the target market includes students on less advanced courses than yours, is the book too introductory? And if the book will appeal to general readers or people outside higher education (such as journalists, politicians, professionals, or administrators in the social sciences), is it sufficiently directed towards academic concerns to be of continuing usefulness to you?

Using Libraries

Universities and polytechnics have widely varying library facilities. The most 'user friendly' libraries are those where:

  (i) there are a large number of books in your subject per student, which increases your chance of finding materials in demand;

 (ii) the indexing system provides flexible access to potentially relevant sources, by author, title keyword, subject category and so on. In general on-line computer search facilities are best, followed a long way behind by micro-fiche systems, with card indexes last;

(iii) books are on open shelves so that you can physically inspect what is available in a particular section, or search for substitutes on nearby shelves if a key source is unavailable;

 (iv) multiple copies of key books can be borrowed or reserved for short periods, but not for so long that they are 'sterilized' and effectively unobtainable;

  (v) the library is fairly specialized in your subject area, so

that you can better understand its organization, and the staff are more likely to offer extended help with queries;
(vi) there are good photocopying facilities which you can operate yourself.

Few libraries will perform well on all these criteria simultaneously, so it is important that you maximize your efficiency in using the resources available to you.

(a) **Pluralize your access to libraries**, using several different sources of supply if you can. Main college libraries are often hard to get to, difficult to borrow books from, and under pressure from many other students. Small libraries in your college, hall of residence or department are useful alternatives where they exist. They normally stock course-related material and let you borrow books for a short time. A second-best book which you can borrow may be more useful than a priority text that you have to read in the main library. And if you cannot find the source you want, alternatives are easier to uncover in a small library than in a large one.

Students often neglect public libraries, but in major towns they normally have very reasonable stocks in the humanities and the social sciences, both for borrowing and in their reference sections. In a city like Birmingham, the central library dwarfs most higher education libraries in terms of its stocks and reader services. Unless you live on a distant campus, always join the main public library in your college town and explore its possibilities. If you have several weeks' notice of when you need books, however specialized, public libraries can usually get them for you on interlibrary loan. Similarly, extended loan facilities are often useful for borrowing basic textbooks for long periods.

(b) **Invest some time in finding out how your main libraries work.** Take the library tour for new students in your first year. Make a note of the main categories of the classification system relevant to your course. In both the Library of Congress and the Dewey systems, material tends to be split between several locations, whatever specific subject you want information on. You probably understand how to use a file card index already, but micro-fiche readers and on-line computer terminals offer much more rapid and flexible access by author names, title, and classification category. If you cannot find a particular book, has the author written anything similar? If you cannot find the author you want, look up keywords which might be included in relevant titles by other authors. Similarly check other entries in the reference category of a missing book for alternative sources on the same or connected themes. For articles, volumes of abstracts summarize the content of each year's journal papers in a discipline. Each article is described in around 150 words and the keywords in the title are usually cross-indexed in quite a sophisticated way, allowing you to find out quickly what has been written on a subject in the last few years. You should learn how to use the volumes of abstracts relevant to your course by your second year.

(c) **Do not depend entirely on references suggested in reading lists.** You may not be able to find many suggested sources because material is already being used, or has disappeared. Equally there may well be occasions when you feel that a lecturer is being over-restrictive in the follow-up material suggested. For example, if a course is being taught without attention to alternative viewpoints you need to have some idea of how to find material written from a different perspective.

When you are not exactly sure what is available or what you are looking for, checking book indexes or journal abstracts is only the first stage of finding alternative sources. Unless you can inspect an item directly you can get little idea of its argument. Looking for 'shelf neighbours' of an elusive book is almost always rewarding, since you can make quick assessments of the usefulness of any new sources you uncover (p. 32). For articles, scan the two most important journals in your course subject, particularly for recent material published in the last year or so. Journals which include short abstracts of articles are the most useful. In some disciplines there are specialized short-article journals with papers limited to around 3,000 words, which are more accessible for student readers.

If you have more time to find sources, Appendix 1 lists the two or three journals in each discipline in the humanities and social sciences which carry the most comprehensive reviews of new books. Reviews can direct you quickly to new sources, or give you a 'second opinion' about the value of a book you have already found for yourself. Any reasonably important work should be covered, but journals' coverage can have gaps because reviewers fail to deliver copy, or because a book is too student-orientated or falls into the concerns of another discipline. British, North American and West European journals comprehensively review books published in their country of origin, but have much patchier coverage of materials published elsewhere. Similarly, where there are both general and more specialized journals in a discipline area, there may be an implicit division of labour between journals in which books they select for review.

2.2 'GUTTING' LITERATURE AND USING SOURCES EFFECTIVELY

Once you have assembled some literature for an assignment, your primary concern is how to get the most out of it in the limited time available. In higher education this is a far more difficult task than at school, because your materials are much more diverse in character. Although you may have some first-year courses with just one or two textbooks, finals courses in the humanities and social sciences typically require you to tackle widely varying materials – such as intermediate texts, journal articles, research monographs, major literary or philosophical texts, diaries or correspondence collections, government policy statements, pieces of legislation, newspaper articles, pamphlets, replica manuscripts, and so on.

In addition, the reasons why you read materials in higher education are very different, depending on where you are in your course, whether you are completing an assignment or reading for background information, what the 'status' of your source is, and how much you already know about the subject involved. The reading advice in study skills books almost universally assumes that you are trying to understand a core textbook from a basis of complete ignorance. In practice you may have no sources which justify the intensive reading appropriate for a core text. You may already know much of the material contained in a source, because you have consulted several other books or papers on the topic. Study skills books also assume that you are searching for the most basic information and ideas in your sources. But again, you may be skimming a book or paper for those aspects of an author's argument which are most distinctive, for the icing on the cake rather than its bottom layers.

Most study skills books (and some students!) are hypnotized by two aspects of reading – how fast you can do it, and how to make exhaustive notes on the material covered. Both preoccupations in my view miss the central difficulty encountered by students in higher education – how to read with questions in mind.

Reading Interrogatively

Once you recognize that the status and character of your literature sources and the reasons why you are reading them both vary widely, you need to get away from focusing too single-mindedly on what authors are trying to say, and instead focus on what you are trying to get out of a source. The key questions to ask are as follows.

(a) **What do I know already?** You will very rarely start reading any source with a blank canvas. Usually you have a good deal of basic information already, from lectures or classes, from earlier background reading, or from basic texts which you have purchased. The danger in conventional methods of reading and note-taking is that by emphasizing understanding and recording the author's thought, getting down the main ideas, and so on, you may spend valuable time re-reading and recording material you already know. Many authors and sources express similar basic ideas for much of the time, although in different ways. You need to be alert to those occasions when what an author is saying differs from your existing knowledge only in surface features. Typically the ideas involved may be very well expressed, in a vocabulary and style much more sophisticated than your own. In some humanities and social science subjects, style and quality of expression are important in their own right, especially in primary sources. But with most secondary material it is vital not to be so hypnotized by the ways in which authors say things that you busily copy down material which is already familiar.

(b) **What am I looking for in this source, what do I think I need?** Normally you should be consulting literature to find material relevant to a specific question for an essay, class paper, or other written assignment. Keeping that question in view while reading is essential because the likelihood is that it is not identical with the author's interests when writing the book or article. Hence you are characteristically in the business of recognizing potentially relevant material and adapting what the author is saying to fit your different purposes. Even when you are reading a course textbook, by no means everything you encounter is going to be relevant for your concerns. Some material will be too basic to include in an essay, since your teacher or tutor will assume that you know it and will not expect to see it reproduced (pp. 146–7). A great deal of material will be too detailed, even if it is directly 'relevant' to your essay focus. In a 200-page book there will be far more detail about a topic than you can conceivably use in a 6-page essay, even if it deals with exactly the same subject.

(c) **What is useful or different in this source, given my existing knowledge and my interests?** When you begin reading in a subject area you may be looking for authors' key ideas and systematically presented basic information. But as you build up your understanding, you may now be looking for controversies, areas of dispute or disagreement, new angles or 'wrinkles' in the presentation of ideas, particularly salient statements of an intellectual position, important quotations, different empirical results or evidence, and so on. Reading interrogatively involves being able to recognize and to home in on precisely the kind of specialized material in the new literature which you so far lack, while skimming over more prosaic or unexceptional areas of the author's thought.

Of course, within this overall orientation of reading with questions in mind, there is still a need to vary your reading approach across three different types of sources. First, some core textbooks (perhaps including a good deal of technical material) need to be systematically studied. Second, there are many situations where the literature consists of diverse secondary sources, each of which sheds light on only one aspect of a topic. Finally there are primary texts or materials where you need to appreciate a complex argument as a whole.

Studying Textbooks: Active Reading

Normally reading is quite a passive activity. For example, if you are tackling a good novel you will start at page 1 and carry on to the end in a single sequence set entirely by the author. Because your role as a reader is minimal, this style of reading is very inappropriate for complex educational materials at degree level, even if you are certain that your source is a core text which you must systematically understand. If you take a great many notes as you go along, you may become more actively engaged with the material, rather than just scanning and trying to understand page after page. But even for very comprehensive note-takers a single slog through a book is unlikely to be an efficient use of time or to generate much understanding.

Active reading essentially involves shifting towards a more sophisticated, multi-stage reading process, one which emphasizes several runs through the material. You take bearings in advance of your main effort at comprehension. Then you split up your main reading effort into manageable tasks, and set yourself some kind of rough timetable for completing these tasks. Finally you reassess your understanding when you have covered the material once through in depth. Active reading is iterative, stressing the need to shift back and forth between scanning the text and assessing your understanding of what you have read. Active reading is also selective: a search period narrows down your focus of attention before you put concentrated effort into trying to master material.

Most textbooks have a developed set of 'planning devices' which can help you plan a reading strategy, such as contents lists (the fuller the better); an introduction explaining in what sequences you can read chapters; and any study advice or objectives which the author gives readers on how to proceed within each chapter. 'Orientating devices' are features of books which help you carry out your reading strategy, including headings and subheadings used in the text (especially their size and appearance); running heads at the top of each page; section numbers (which indicate the skeleton structure of an author's argument); the index (assuming there is a good one, this can give immediate access to precisely specified subject matter); any descriptions given in-text by the author (e.g. designating particular passages as 'essential reading', while other material is skippable, included in an appendix, and so on). Waller (1977) emphasizes that paying explicit attention to these devices can make books much more accessible than otherwise.

One very formal set of procedures for encouraging active reading which makes use of these various planning and orientating devices is the so-called SQ3R approach. These initials sound forbidding but simply stand for a sequence of five operations which readers are advised to perform: survey (S), question (Q), read, recall and review (the 3 'R's).

(1) **To survey a text**, try to get an overall idea of what it is about. Read the introduction (or preface, or foreword, it may be called any of these), look at the contents page, and then leaf through the book looking at chapter headings and subsections, and reading any end-of-chapter summaries. Similarly if you are only surveying an article or a particular chapter you might read the abstract (if there is one), glance through the piece, read the introductory or concluding paragraphs and look at any diagrams, tables or illustrations.

(2) **The question phase** entails framing some queries about the book or chapter on the basis of your survey, asking which are the key concepts to understand, how they relate to each other, and which are the central arguments that need to be mastered. Make sure you jot your queries down on paper.

(3) **The reading stage** involves working through part of the source methodically from beginning to end without making notes, concentrating on understanding what the author is saying. Obviously you should do this only section by section in a textbook, not from beginning to

end of the book. Even when working through a paper or single chapter, it is usually appropriate to do so section by section.

(4) **Recall** is the stage where you pause in your reading to summarize your own understanding, particularly by jotting down notes of what the author's main points were. Most 'how to study' manuals see this stage as critical. For example, Rowntree (1982, p. 59) recommends as a general rule spending around half your total reading time on recall. But he suggests that this ratio will need to be much greater (perhaps 80–90 per cent) when you are trying to learn how to use formulae, graphs or the technical apparatus encountered in some social sciences. By contrast, where material has a narrative form (e.g. history, biography or literature) the recall phase is less all-important, perhaps accounting for only a fifth of overall reading time.

(5) In the much briefer **review stage** the key thing is to compare what you have recalled with the text itself, looking for important points you missed, checking whether you now have answers to queries defined at the question stage, and making sure that your notes accurately capture what the author said. In many ways reviewing is like resurveying the text from the basis of your notes or other recall material.

If you have not previously come across the SQ3R method then you may well find it valuable to give it a try. Some critics see the approach as over-regimented, too fussy and likely to hinder some students' development (Main, 1980). It is most useful in tackling big chunks of text which you simply have to master to understand a subject. By definition, it is only worthwhile applying this intensive, time-consuming reading to materials which are very basic to your studies.

'Gutting' Literature: Secondary Texts

Writing nearly 200 years ago the German poet Goethe complained: 'Certain books seem to have been written, not in order to afford us any instruction, but merely for the purpose of letting us know that their authors knew something' (Goethe, 1958 edn, p. 272). The contemporary 'information explosion' and the growth of the academic professions have only worsened the problem. Publishing books and papers has become a major means of professional advancement. With larger student audiences and library markets, the quality controls on academic books and journals have been under pressure. Small production runs for high-priced books selling to libraries have transformed the economics of specialized publishing. All these factors have lengthened reading lists, diversified sources of information, and worsened student overload. The very variable quality of published output places a premium on being critical in your reading, while its volume emphasizes the need to make rapid appreciations of whether a source is useful and in what respect.

'Gutting' literature is simply an extreme form of active, interrogative reading which copes with these pressures by extracting a kernel of usable information from a source as quickly as possible. A corollary of this attitude is that you are not concerned with the overall integrity of a book or article. Much of what the author says is ignored. You only tap into those sections of the source which meet your needs, before moving on to another source. Critics argue that the approach can be misleading, causing you to misconstrue or misrepresent what authors mean. Certainly any particular passage needs to be set in the context of a book or article's overall argument, as far as this is possible. But the general academic prejudice of frowning on selective reading is unfounded.

On many topics where you are dealing with a plethora of secondary texts or articles, gutting the literature is a perfectly rational way of proceeding, so long as it is fairly sensitively done. Typically your first task is to establish the 'status' of a source, deciding how much effort it will repay. Check what details are given about the author, where she works, whom she seems to be influenced by, and what she says about the purpose in writing the book in the preface, foreword or introduction. Then use the contents page and index to search for material which is immediately relevant for your concerns. Having identified useful passages, search back for the most appropriate place to begin reading in depth, which is usually the start of the text subsection involved. A rapid survey of preceding material is usually valuable to set the section in context, then the section is skimmed to get a general idea of its argument, before being carefully read (with any notes probably taken simultaneously since the section will not be overlong). For articles, read the abstract and conclusions, skim the paper as a whole, and read intensively the most relevant sections.

In general, if you encounter obstacles – such as a passage which is incomprehensible at first sight, an unfamiliar formula, complex data presentation, or a difficult diagram – the best rule is to go round the difficulty on a first run through, in the hope that a later part of the text clarifies its importance or meaning. This *blitzkreig* style is especially appropriate to the selective reading of secondary texts because you cannot assume (as you might with a course textbook or a primary source) that every section builds up into a single essential argument. Many authors introduce difficult material into their writing which it is not strictly necessary to understand if you are to follow their argument. Frequently in the social sciences complex statistics, mathematical notation or graphs and diagrams may be introduced but then subsequently not really used in the analysis. Often where authors state an argument in terms of an algebraic formula, they go on to give an 'ordinary language' interpretation of the steps involved and the conclusions reached. Similarly in the humanities, quite complex theories or conceptual elements can be set out in the early parts of books, which do not perceptibly influence the presentation of empirical material or the practical application to literary analysis in the rest of the text.

Therefore by-passing points of difficulty until you have established their significance will not necessarily jeopardize your chance of understanding what follows. But if it does then you have no option but to go back and 'storm' the original problem which is holding up your progress. You may want to work through it using the SQ3R approach if it is a long passage. If the key section is quite short, and you have already surveyed it, then a single straight read-through may be most appropriate. But for the reasons I have explained, do not do this time-consuming (and possibly brain-numbing) task before you have to.

Once you have covered the most relevant passages for your concerns, a final stage in gutting a source is quickly to survey subsequent material, including concluding summaries or chapters. Again the idea is to check that your use and interpretation of the extract which you have read in depth does not do violence to the author's intentions and overall argument.

Handling Primary Texts

Formal approaches to reading like the SQ3R method are much less use when you are handling primary source materials – such as a novel, play or long poem; a major work in philosophy or a significant volume of social thought; a tightly constructed technical or mathematical argument; or a complex piece of legislation. Similarly methods of 'gutting' literature are inappropriate for three reasons. First, reading a piece of text once through intensively, and coming 'cold' to it (without preconceptions or advance knowledge of its contents), can be crucial in some contexts. In literature, for example, your first encounter with a novel or a poem is an important source of information about the piece and about your own reactions to it. Second, it is usually important in understanding this kind of text that you respect its integrity. Appreciating the overall tone, atmosphere and intention of a novel or a piece of philosophy is crucial in understanding the text, not an incidental or dispensable luxury in your reading. Similarly in tackling a piece of legislation, questions about the 'spirit' of the law or reading the intentions of the law-makers into the potentially ambiguous text are fundamental activities. Third, it may be important to keep very large parts of the entire argument in view in order to understand what comes next. Where a case is built up in a strictly hierarchical, cumulative fashion – as in a lengthy piece of legal or philosophical argument – there may be no viable alternative to working through it carefully from beginning to end, perhaps taking extensive notes en route.

However, it is often possible to short-circuit some of the slog otherwise involved in reading *large* primary sources by using the following procedures.

(a) **A fairly fast first read through the text** is a good idea. I noted above that there are circumstances where you may not want to make much use of look-ahead or orientating devices. For example, skimming a novel before settling down to read it properly could mean that you deprive yourself of a sense of build-up, tension, surprise or shock which the author has crafted to create. But equally in these circumstances the author has not written the book to be comprehensively studied and annotated, so that quite a fast read through may come closer to giving you a feel for the writer's intentions than crawling along making notes as you go. With larger, more complex and more technical works an initial read through by itself is not going to give you a firm grasp on the argument, although it may let you get an overall idea of its canvas. Where the scale of a work means that you cannot digest it at one sitting, try the suggestion made in Chapter 1 on background reading: put it in your bathroom and work through a few pages each night.

Since you will almost always need to buy copies of primary texts, it is probably better not to make notes on your first read through, but instead to sideline or highlight your copy of the text directly, perhaps keeping a very brief running log of passages where you have made comments or which struck you as particularly important. One of the most important roles for such a running log is to note down any interconnections between different passages in the text – for example, places where an author seems to be contradicting himself, specifying or expanding an original point, or putting a new gloss on what was said earlier. Properly constructed this log can play much the same role as an index does in a modern academic book. Hence it is particularly valuable where you are reading a novel, a play, a legal statute or an older philosophical text – all of which rarely have any index system.

(b) Where you are tackling a large primary text, you should quickly **consult some secondary sources** – such as literary criticism about a play or novel, or secondary exegesis and discussion of a major piece of philosophy or social theory. The idea here is to avoid approaching a bulky text in detail with no idea of what you are looking for. Many students feel that it is somehow unethical or undesirable to look at what other academics have said about a primary text before they have fully mastered it themselves. They feel that if they can just sit down and read the main text through methodically, then in some way they will have formed 'their own' appreciation of it first. This can be true of small texts, such as poems. But with large primary sources the text is often too long and complex to be grasped so easily. The first read through may just be very confusing. You may understand each individual part as you read it, but yet have no real sense of the interrelationship of the parts or their significance for the text as a whole. In this situation reading some secondary treatments of the main text can sensitize you to the existence of different interpretations from the outset, so that you can pick out relevant passages as you work through on your own. It provides you with a set of questions to keep in mind, so that you can still read the primary text interrogatively.

(c) **More detailed study of the text** should be carried out in a selective fashion. It should focus on particular topics and problems within a properly fleshed-out context, based both on a reading of the text as a whole and on some acquaintance with the secondary literature. This kind of selective reading will inevitably be iterative or recursive, involving you in tracking backwards and forwards between interrelated sections, familiarizing yourself in depth with their argument or construction. You will also begin matching up secondary analysis with your own readings of sections of the primary text.

In literary subjects your study will inevitably depart in some way from the primary text's sequencing of materials – since 'studying' a text is a specialized act carried out for distinctive purposes. So long as you have the experience of your own initial reading to draw on, to remind you of the author's intentions for those experiencing the text, there is no reason to worry that your study procedure is an illegitimate one. Film versions of novels, or live performances of poems and drama, can help renew or reinforce your initial reading experience – even if the new medium will naturally introduce distinctive elements of its own which are not present in the primary source *qua* text.

2.3 TAKING NOTES

Taking systematic notes has several major advantages. They provide a personal record of materials which you have encountered, a 'paper memory' which is a good deal more secure than information which you have only filed mentally. Most notes are quite drastic summaries of the original materials, and the way in which you accomplish this compression, choosing materials to include or leave out, can help you work out your own ideas. Notes can be reused much more easily than the original text because they already express your own understanding. They can be added to or rewritten later on, an especially useful characteristic in revision. In principle then, reading and note-taking with questions in mind could be an active learning process with cumulative dividends.

However, there are also four major difficulties with note-taking. First it considerably lengthens the time needed to work systematically through a source, time which you might not be able to afford. Second, unless you make a special effort to focus on your own understanding, it is more normal for note-taking to become a passive form of learning, writing out other people's ideas in a structure determined by their concerns and priorities. If taking systematic notes erodes your thinking or writing time for an essay, your argument can easily seem very derivative or fail to address the precise question asked. Third, there can be a lack of fit between the way you make notes and the kind of information which you want to record, which could make note-taking inefficient. For example, many people find it hard to combine selective reading of a book or an article with a conventional approach to note-taking which focuses on comprehensively reproducing an author's argument (see pp. 41–2 below). Fourth, you obviously lose much information at the note-taking stage, which may be important for writing an assignment or during later revision. Very full notes minimize this sacrifice but make your role even more passive, take longer to do, and are almost as difficult to reuse as the original text.

Many students worry a great deal about taking or not taking notes while they are gathering information. Study skills books uniformly suggest that systematic note-taking is an essential study habit. If you do not take a great many notes, you may well feel very guilty about your apparently 'scrappy' habits. In fact, there is no systematic research evidence of a close connection between extensive note-taking and overall academic performance (Gibbs, 1981, pp. 58–60). It seems highly plausible that a large stock of well-executed notes is an advantage for most students. But the converse is not true: many students who do well in higher education do not place a great deal of emphasis on note-taking, perhaps especially in the humanities and the less technical social sciences. Instead they put their efforts into writing a lot of essays, where they learn new material by incorporating it directly into their own pattern of argument.

When to Make Notes

Because there are pros and cons of note-taking which will vary in importance from one person to another, you have to make your own decision about how many and what kind of notes you need. However, it is useful to pose a few questions before you launch into note-taking.

(a) **Do you have any alternative means of making a record of the materials involved?** If you can afford to buy books or to photocopy articles or chapters, then sidelining or highlighting passages and making marginal comments of your own is a quicker and easier way to pinpoint key arguments, while retaining the full text for later re-reading if necessary. The less you acquire a stockpile of personal study materials in this way, the more important it is to make notes of what you read.

(b) **Can you realistically get access to these materials again?** You are unlikely ever to re-read most books or articles which you use in libraries, because of the initial difficulties in finding the source, and the pressure to move on to other topics. Similarly you normally cannot rerun lectures (or broadcasts) if you missed parts of what was said. Taping lectures simply postpones a solution. Although you can replay the audio tape at difficult points, understanding (let alone transcribing) an hour's talk from a poor recording and without the lecturer's non-verbal cues or any visual aids is often very difficult and always time-consuming.

(c) **Is the source you are using important not just for an immediate assignment, but more generally?** Should you 'invest' in it by taking notes for later use? When generating information you are primarily looking for material to use in essays. But especially if you have to sit end-of-course exams you may worry about taking broader notes which could be useful in revising. The difficulty here lies in anticipating your future needs effectively. For example, research suggests that most students who make notes rarely re-read them, perhaps because they have a better understanding of their subject by the time they come to do final revision than when they first encountered materials. So do not 'overinvest' on an off-chance that in one or two years' time the source will turn out to be useful.

(d) **Will making notes appreciably advance your understanding of a source?** As the SQ3R reading approach suggests, making notes can be a very important activity in boosting your understanding of technical materials or very complex arguments. Ideally, try not to make notes on your first read through – doing it on the recall phase makes it much easier to select what to include or leave out.

(e) **Is it important to record your own reactions and queries as you encounter a new topic or source of materials?** Nothing is more fleeting, or more difficult to reinspect, than your own thinking at different stages of getting to grips with a subject. Most professional writers religiously make a note of their ideas and stray thoughts whenever they have them. Keeping a filepad or notebook to hand can often make the difference between vaguely recognizing that you have had a good idea (which then proves hard to pin down or recall), and providing yourself with a foundation for some original writing and argument. A record of this kind is invaluable in the difficult stage of 'generating ideas' during essay writing (pp. 84–5).

(f) **What style of notes is appropriate for the source you are using and the material which you want to record?** Notes are a purely personal study aid. Do not feel constrained to make them in any particular format unless it fits your needs. Some students inherit from their schooldays a fear that their private notes will be inspected at some stage by teachers, something which virtually never happens in higher education.

You may find it helpful to follow a general method of note-taking, such as the two procedures outlined below. But these are simply suggestions, which may be less effective than your own personalized approach.

Conventional Note-Taking

The time-honoured model of note-taking given in most existing advice books emphasizes reproducing an outline plan of a book's or a lecture's argument.

> Your notebook must show:
> a. The author's main ideas and any important supporting detail.
> b. The logical plan of his argument (the hierarchy of ideas).
> . . . Get a skeleton for your outline from the author's headings (if he has used them). Expand each heading into a sentence containing the main idea of the section or sub-section it belongs to.
> . . . Having picked out the main ideas (of sections, sub-sections, and paragraphs), you indent them from the margin, according to their relative importance. Main ideas start at the margin. Second-order items are indented by, say, half an inch. Third-order items go in by another half inch, and so on. Don't indent too little, or the relationships won't be clear.
>
> (Rowntree, 1982, pp. 114, 119–20)

This simple sort of procedure has a good deal to commend it for short passages where there are lots of main ideas all at one level. But in longer pieces of text, especially where there is one starter idea, you soon find the indentation system going awry and having to be supplemented with copious underlinings and other emphasis devices. Much the same problems arise where you are using numbers or letters to indicate the beginning of sections, subsections, and paragraphs. It helps to follow a standard format for lettering and numbering notes which you can become accustomed to using (and to interpreting on re-reading). For example, the most flexible and extendable numbering system uses multiple decimal points, so that the first subsection of section 2 is numbered 2.1, and in turn its first paragraph becomes 2.1.1, and so on. More cumbersomely, you might use capital letters for main sections, arabic numerals for subsections, lower-case letters for paragraphs, and small roman numerals for component points (giving a sequence such as A.1.a.i).

Sorting out concepts or topics into higher and lower order elements is most useful in technical subjects, but even here it may not be straightforward. The most basic ideas may not be the ones which are given the most explicit treatment in the literature, or talked about for the longest period of time. For example, micro-economics textbooks tend to introduce the idea of a 'market' quite quickly, and then spend a great deal of time discussing the ways to draw demand and supply curves showing how much of a good will be produced and sold at different prices. Whether such curves can be validly drawn in fact depends on whether a market actually exists in a particular area of social life. Thus the demand and supply curve concepts are premissed on the market concept. In most cases textbooks will offer clues to this sort of interconnection in their arrangement of material, with higher order concepts being introduced first and lower order ideas subsequently. But it is often easy to miss the higher order concepts – they can be introduced quickly as preliminaries before the author gets into the meat of the analysis. So the argument structure and the relative emphasis which should be given to different ideas may not be the same.

In the humanities and less technical social sciences, by contrast, overall 'theme' ideas are usually more prominent, reappearing at various points in the analysis as linking or tone-setting elements. But since the nature of these theme ideas varies more markedly, they can appear rather diffuse. Themes can be indivdual concepts, metaphors or analogies (sometimes very extended in form), or substantive propositions and arguments. Conventional note-taking may not work well in these subjects because it assumes a single hierarchy of ideas which is actually rather a rare occurrence in degree-level work. Hierarchic patterns of note-taking cannot easily cope with the multiple and complex relationships between concepts and topics. Here more graphic methods of representing the connections within bundles of ideas are valuable.

Patterned Notes

One good way to cope with more varied materials is to use some jottings or diagrams in your notes. It is often easier to organize your ideas in the two-dimensional space of a sheet of paper, rather than the one-dimensional ordering produced by simple lists, or chronologies, or the sequence of ideas in the textbook. The most basic kind of visual representation is a series of boxes used to highlight clusters of associated notions with arrows between them to indicate relationships.

Patterned notes go one stage futher in developing a flexible alternative to conventional note-taking (Buzan, 1974). You place the central idea of a piece of text or a lecture in a prominent box in the middle of your page. Lines radiate out from this box for derivative or related ideas, arguments or pieces of empirical evidence. You can write comments on these lines where the relationship between the two concepts needs to be clarified or remembered. From each of the second-order concepts further branching lines carry on the argument. Figure 2.1 shows a set of patterned notes for the argument of this section (2.3). In general the more important an idea, the closer it lies to the centre of the page, while the most detailed points are clustered around the periphery. This approach is very useful because in much of the material you are reading you will need to write down and remember more about points of detail than you do about major concepts, with which you are already familiar. Thus the centre of your page may be sparsely annotated but as you work out along the branches so you record more material, quotations, and so on. Patterned notes fit much better with selective, 'skim' reading than does the conventional approach with its emphasis upon comprehensiveness. Compared with traditional notes they need a minimum of text, which reduces the risk that they will be wordy paraphrases of the text, article or lecture involved.

Taking Notes in Lectures

Most students confront a basic dilemma when a lecturer does not issue notes. You can assemble some sort of record by scribbling down as much as possible without really understanding the lecturer's argument. Or you can concentrate on listening while your notes necessarily become rather restricted. Even if a lecture is easy to follow and very

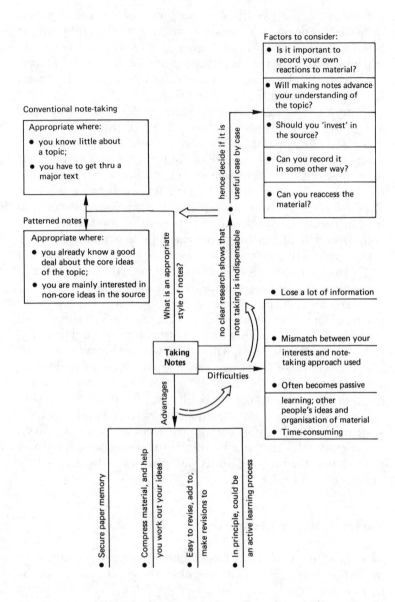

Figure 2.1: A set of patterned notes summarizing the argument of section 2.3

useful, the nagging doubt whether you will have a full or useful residue of what is said affects most of us at some stage.

One way out of this dilemma is to pair up with a fellow student whose interests and level of academic performance are quite similar to your own. Both of you attend all the lectures but do different things in alternate weeks. One of you concentrates on following the lecturer's train of thought, while the other makes fairly full notes (with plenty of space for additions). After the lecture, say during the coffee break, you go quickly through the notes adding in any material which the note-taker missed, and discussing what was meant at points of difficulty. Write down these ideas plus your own reactions directly on the notes you have. Then get a photocopy of the revised record so you both have the notes, and next week swap roles. This kind of co-operative effort can work only with students of similar interests and abilities, otherwise you can end up resenting the work you put in compared with the sketchy notes which your partner provides in return.

Summary of Suggestions: Generating Information

1. Faced with long, unannotated reading lists: ask teachers to indicate priorities; read modern books and literature review articles first; read student-orientated books before the research literature (p. 23).

2. When buying books, always assess them yourself; do not buy on recommendations only. Make sure you acquire some up-to-date core books for each course. Buy unchanging materials second-hand (p. 23).

3. Use several different libraries if you can. Invest some time in understanding your main library. Do not rely solely on reading list suggestions but be ready to look constructively for material on your own (p. 24).

4. Always read with questions in mind, asking: What do I know already? What do I need to know? What is new or different in this source? (p. 28).

5. Read actively, in several stages, skimming to get a general view of the source before studying it in a more concentrated way, and then periodically assessing your understanding. Make full use of the planning and orientating devices in books (p. 30).

6. If you have to master a major textbook or difficult article, try out the SQ3R approach (i.e. survey, question, read, recall, review), to see if it helps your understanding (p. 31).

7. To 'gut' secondary literature: establish the status of the source; use the index, contents page or skim reading to identify sections needing detailed study; establish their context; read key sections intensively, by-passing initial obstacles until it is clear they cannot be neglected; finally, survey subsequent material swiftly to check that your interpretation of the key passages is correct (p. 33).

8. Tackle long primary texts by: a fairly fast first read through; consulting some secondary sources which discuss the text; and conducting more detailed study selectively in an iterative way (p. 35).

9. Weigh up the pros and cons of note-taking, and check for each source: Can you make a record in some other way? Can you reaccess the material? Should you 'invest' time in studying it for future benefits? Will note-taking aid your understanding? Is it important to record your reactions? (p. 39).

10. A conventional note-taking style is most appropriate if you know little about a subject and are studying a textbook with a clear hierarchy of ideas (p. 41).

11. Where your existing knowledge is more extensive, you may be reading more selectively and be interested less in the author's core ideas than in more peripheral angles and insights: here patterned notes are more appropriate (p. 42).

12. If making notes while following lectures is difficult, pair up with a colleague to divide the tasks between you and produce a joint record of what is said (p. 43).

3 Analysing Concepts and Theories

Reading Guide

Improving your handling of concepts and theories involves:

1. Clarifying the meanings of individual concepts.
2. Analysing the interrelationship between several concepts in the same area of thought.
3. Understanding overall theoretical controversies in your subject.

The first two sections introduce a number of key ideas, such as the uses of brainstorming and of 'lateral thinking', which are important in essay writing (Chapter 4) and revising for exams (Chapter 6). Experienced students can skim section 3.3, although the ideas here are also important.

3.1 CLARIFYING INDIVIDUAL CONCEPTS

Only by using words in line with an established language can we communicate our thoughts to others or understand their messages in return. Language embodies an accumulated pattern of usage built up over a long period and by frequent repetition of an idea. 'A language is, on the one hand, little affected by the use individuals make of it; but, on the other hand, it almost entirely patterns the character of what is thought, felt, or said by those using it' (Marshall McCluan, 1959, p. 340).

In the humanities and social sciences a concern with terms, concepts and meanings is fundamental to degree-level work. You are expected to use words and ideas precisely; to be sensitive to nuances or fluctuations in meaning; and to be aware of how ideas might be connected innovatively. These qualities are interpreted as fundamental indicators of intellectual development, not as tangential or dispensable study skills. The analysis of concepts, ideas and terminology in different aspects is a key rationale of disciplines such as philosophy, theology, linguistics, literary criticism, social and political theory, and anthropology. Even in the least literary subjects (such as accounting or macroeconomics), alternative ways of constructing and interrelating technical concepts remain central points of debate.

There is a small set of immediately useful techniques for handling concepts which you may want to integrate into your own academic work. Despite the diversity and richness of the conceptual analysis in most coursework, only a tiny proportion of this material can easily rub off and be incorporated into your own ways of thinking and studying. The methods suggested here are suitable for use while writing short essays, taking part in class discussions, or revising for examinations across many disciplines. Direct methods of clarifying individual concepts are by far the most familiar; faced with a problematic concept they look for synonyms or definitions. Indirect methods are probably more useful at degree level; they work by situating a problematic concept within a whole field of ideas.

Direct Methods of Defining Meanings

The conventional western way of tackling intellectual difficulties is by a frontal analysis, focusing on a tightly defined area and puzzling away at the problem until light dawns. This one-directional approach is a type of 'vertical' reasoning; it assumes that concentrated attention will suffice to clarify what is at issue. Confronted by a problematic concept or term, we proceed by comparing alternative definitions of the word, perhaps looking also at the setting where the idea is used. Most people tackling a written assignment stare at any clearly academic concept and try to work out what it means, including how it is used in the question itself. Concepts specific to one academic discipline should be quite extensively described in a specialist subject dictionary (see Appendix 1).

Unless the concept is an exclusively technical one, a brief definition will rarely clear up all aspects of its meaning.

Especially in the humanities and social sciences, key terms have numerous academic and ordinary language meanings, each of which may evoke a different penumbra of theoretical or ideological notions (section 3.3). Many of the most problematic ideas used in essay questions are ordinary language terms which express a particular evaluation or description. Of course, they can be looked up in a conventional dictionary, but since they also have multiple meanings, the problem of choosing between interpretations may not be much reduced.

Definitions have a fairly restricted value anyway. Most attempts to specify the meaning of a term involve a hunt for synonyms. A more familiar substitute word (or several substitutes) replaces the concept whose meaning is unclear. There is a great deal of point in 'putting things in your own words', because we need to know considerably more than a bare meaning in order to use terms successfully. You need to be able to control shades of meaning precisely, to have a sense of occasion about when a word is appropriate or inappropriate, to be sensitive to its wider connotations – all of which is much easier if you are using familiar terminology. Nonetheless synonym hunting is difficult because it commonly involves ransacking your brains against an empty canvas, picking up individual alternative words or meanings and comparing them one by one with the problem term. The quest for definitions can easily become overprecise. Looking for a single substitute for the isolated problem term risks rejecting as irrelevant many partially or tangentially involved meanings which could otherwise open up interesting avenues of thought.

Indirect Methods of Defining Meanings

Some writers argue that 'lateral thinking' can help overcome the tunnel vision of 'vertical reasoning'. For example, de Bono (1970) points out the existence of a class of puzzles which seem brain-numbingly difficult to most people struggling to find an answer. Yet when once the answer is reached or explained to them, the problem seems utterly straightforward, and the same people wonder how they could ever have found it hard to see the solution. If you have not tried a lateral-thinking puzzle before, de Bono (1971, pp. 172–6) uses a simple but very useful example: take an ordinary small picture postcard, about half the size of this page, and cut a hole in it big enough to get your entire head through. Try it yourself with the right size piece of paper and a pair of scissors and see how long you take to work out an answer. Try not to cheat either: a 'hole' here means a gap surrounded by continuous uncut paper, with no joins in it. (For two possible solutions see pp. 76–7.)

These problems which become 'transparent' when solved are simply explained. There is nothing intrinsically very difficult about the task which originally faces us. But our established ways of thinking can quite easily create a very substantial barrier to seeing the solution. Because we are used to approaching problems in familiar ways and a new conundrum does not fit in, we experience the puzzle as very difficult, perhaps even insoluble. But when the answer is explained, we see how to conceptualize the issue differently and the problem disappears, perhaps becoming difficult even to perceive any more. If you cannot see the solution to one of these 'perceptual' puzzles early on, no amount of brain-cudgelling about the problem is likely to overcome your 'block' and let you see it differently. Thus 'lateral thinking' involves deliberately trying to relax preconceived ways of seeing problems. You search for alternative images which might produce a *gestalt* shift in the puzzle's appearance and hence illuminate a way forward.

Whether lateral thinking can be taught or inculcated in the ways which de Bono suggests, and what use this might be, remain controversial. Most intellectual problems are initially much vaguer and less closely specified than the normal lateral-thinking puzzles. But it certainly is possible to liberalize the ways in which we work through problems and to become more sensitive to the limits of vertical reasoning. The potential for improving flexibility in academic thinking is probably greatest at the stage of clarifying concepts and generating ideas. Most students at some stage experience difficulties in perceiving 'obvious' ideas or connections relevant to a question or topic. If you initially conceptualize an issue in an over-restrictive way, this can prevent later insights from developing, committing you to a single track of thinking. Indirect methods of clarifying concepts instead create a whole field of ideas within which the wider meanings and implications of a problem term can be appreciated. Five steps are useful.

(a) **Place the concept in its 'universe'** (a term derived from set theory), i.e. ask what type of idea a term refers to. For example, democracy is a type of political system, neurosis is a type of psychological condition, black is a type of colour, and so on.

(b) **Search for antonyms to the concept within this universe.** Antonyms are the reverse of synonyms, they are what the problem term is opposed to. The idea here is a typical lateral-thinking notion: that to know what a concept is, one of the best clues is to know what it is not, what the reverse of the concept is or what the concept is most opposed to. Obviously if you have not already specified the universe within which this search for antonyms is to be conducted, then the activity becomes an open-ended one – the category of not being the problem term is enlarged unmanageably to include all kinds of words referring to quite different subjects. But if you have already established that democracy is a type of political system, or that black is a colour, then the range of not-democracy or not-black terms which you have to survey is usually quite restricted.

Most key terms in the social sciences and humanities have several potential antonyms. Even a simple word such as 'black' can be contrasted differently depending on the context. Most people give 'white' as its antonym, but the appropriate contrast might be black/red in accounting and economics, or black vs any other colour in physics (since white light is in fact an amalgam of the whole spectrum of colours, and darkness is the absence of any light of whatever colour). Similarly, if you ask a student audience what is the opposite of democracy, a dazzling array of answers is invariably produced. British students most frequently respond 'totalitarianism', while Americans tend to favour 'communism'. Minorities of people give other answers such as 'fascism' (from people on the political left), 'oligarchy', 'dictatorship', and so on. In each case the responses given reflect an attempt to situate 'democracy' within a dichotomy or polarity. This tendency to construct dichotomies (exhaustive classifications of a subject matter into two parts) is a basic feature of western thought and strongly influences the ways in which all of us see the world. By contrasting a problem term with an unlike term, we gain very considerable insights.

Yet as the ability to generate several antonyms for most terms might suggest, there is an ambiguity in searching for opposites. By the opposite of a term X we should mean the most exhaustive term for not-X, so that we can accurately draw the boundary between X and everything else in the relevant universe (Figure 3.1). However, when we formulate contrasts

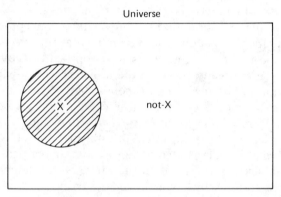

Figure 3.1: An appropriate dichotomy: X and not-X

to guide our use of the X term in ordinary speech, it is very easy to fall victim to a 'false dichotomy', an artificial or exaggerated contrast between X and another term Y, where Y in fact covers only a small proportion of the class of objects or ideas falling into the not-X category (Figure 3.2). For example, the familiar contrast between 'democracy' and 'totalitarianism' is a false dichotomy because totalitarian regimes are a very small subclass of all non-democratic regimes. A totalitarian system aims to control society with a centralized dictatorship by a party and single leader, usually employing systematic terror, in which all areas of social life became politicized and subject to homogenous state direction. But most non-democratic regimes do not go this far. For instance, many dictatorships are military regimes set up when a group of colonels replaces the parliament with their own non-elected government, suppressing political controversy and controlling the press. But very few

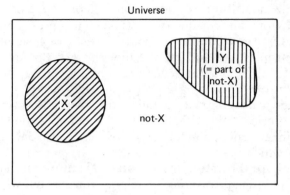

Figure 3.2: A false dichotomy: X and Y

authoritarian regimes attempt in any systematic way to control other aspects of social life (such as business, religion, family life, and so on). Countries as diverse as Yugoslavia, Turkey, South Africa, Chile or Hong Kong are all run non-democratically at present, but none of them are totalitarian regimes.

False dichotomies are usually adopted implicitly, without those involved being very aware of what they are doing. They can be extremely misleading. The totalitarianism/democracy contrast, for example, often leads people into characterizing lapses from democratic procedures as 'steps towards totalitarianism'. In most cases this is not remotely accurate; what is involved are shifts towards authoritarian or dictatorial rule very far removed from any direct connection with totalitarianism. Note also that even if you have an initially correct or plausible definition of a term, you can still systematically misapply it within a false dichotomy later on, unless you have self-consciously worked out what is its correct antonym.

In working out antonyms it is worth bearing in mind some simple prefixes which can be applied to a problem term to generate potential opposites. The 'non-', or 'un-' forms are familiar. Sometimes there may be two prefixes signifying opposites, with different meanings. In economics a 'non-rational' decision is one made on some criterion other than a calculation of costs and benefits: for example, fixing a price for commodities on the basis of religious belief rather than profit maximization. But this 'non-rational' choice may be very far indeed from an 'irrational' decision. The 'pre-' and 'post' prefixes are also important and can generate significantly different questions and lines of thought. For example, is the opposite of 'industrial society' a non-industrial society, a pre-industrial society, or a post-industrial society? Using the non-industrial contrast includes the two latter senses as subcategories, but without any of the implications of an evolutionary or predetermined sequence of development phases which the pre- or post-industrial usages imply.

(c) **Look for the antonyms of potential antonyms.** This step can be of crucial assistance in helping you sort out which of a cluster of potential antonyms for a problem term is the most useful for your purposes. Here you simply ask of each of the alleged opposites of the problem term, what is their opposite in turn. For example, to return to the problem of defining 'democracy', the antonyms of antonyms might be as shown below. The correct antonym in this list is obviously

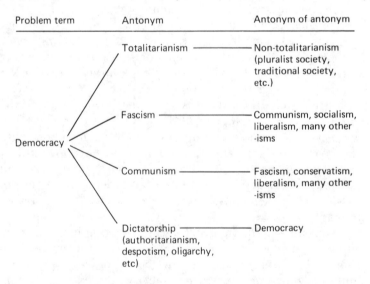

Problem term	Antonym	Antonym of antonym
Democracy	Totalitarianism	Non-totalitarianism (pluralist society, traditional society, etc.)
	Fascism	Communism, socialism, liberalism, many other -isms
	Communism	Fascism, conservatism, liberalism, many other -isms
	Dictatorship (authoritarianism, despotism, oligarchy, etc)	Democracy

'dictatorship', the one whose own opposite is identical with the problem term itself. If the antonym of an antonym leads off in another direction, to a different concept entirely, you have the strongest possible indication that it is potentially misleading.

The antonyms of potential antonyms provide vital indications of where misinterpretations are likely to occur, their scope and direction. These are accordingly vital points to watch in your own use of the problem term.

(d) **Look for unstated 'partner' words.** Most key concepts in the humanities and social sciences, precisely because they are vague or disputed, are often used with specifying words which fix their meaning more precisely. Yet in essay or exam questions partner words are frequently left implicit, partly because the question context may make them unnecessary, partly because teachers may deliberately wish to keep open a wider range of possible student interpretations of the question. Hidden partner words can in fact carry the major part of the burden of specifying a concept. For example, to ask whether a particular work or style is 'art' almost always means, is it 'great art'? Similarly, in the West most common usage of the single term 'democracy' actually means 'liberal democracy' via representative institutions, rather than 'direct democracy' (as in small town meetings) or 'People's democracy' of the East European variety. Lack of attention to unstated partner words can easily enlarge a debate or controversy artificially, in the process making your written assignment less manageable and more confused.

(e) **Explicitly examine different forms of a concept.** Many key concepts, perhaps especially in the social sciences, are used in quite different if still connected ways depending on whether they refer to a given state of affairs or to a process of dynamic change, and depending on whether they are used in an adjectival or a noun form. Sometimes there are several suffixes (such as '-ism' or '-ization' or '-ology') which can be added on to a basic term to connote distinct concepts.

For example, in urban geography and urban sociology the connected ideas of 'urban', 'urbanism' and 'urbanization' frequently appear together. Here 'urban' is an adjective used to denote a town or city-like settlement, or a social condition or process characteristic of such settlements. 'Urbanism' is a noun which sometimes denotes a way of life allegedly characteristic of people in urban settlements, and sometimes an ideology espousing the virtues of living in towns (as opposed to 'anti-urbanism', an ideology of hostility to city living). And 'urbanization' denotes the process by which an increasing proportion of people in a society come to live in 'urban' settlements, or alternatively the process by which urbanism (an urban way of life) becomes generalized throughout the society. There are numerous similar bundles of related terms in many disciplines.

If one element of such a bundle appears in an essay or exam question, it is extremely likely that your response will make some reference to other forms of the basic term. So it is important that you define all of the variants involved explicitly, and sensitize yourself to the conditions under which each is appropriately used. Finally, it is common to find students and some academics using 'long', apparently more impressive versions of basic words inappropriately, especially '-ism' and '-ology' variants. For example, many people write about 'methodology' when they mean 'method', or about 'professionalism' when they mean 'professional', or about 'federalism' when they mean 'federation'. In each case, these pairs of words have quite distinct meanings.

Looking back over the suggestions in this section, you should appreciate that understanding a problem concept is a relatively complex operation. It is not just a matter of looking up an unfamiliar term in some single source. Rather it is a question of sorting out in your own mind how to use the term intelligently and accurately in your writing, building up an overall picture of the concept layer by layer. But with a little practice, concept clarification can become easier and not more difficult by using these suggestions. Problem words are much harder to get to grips with if you have no regular or reliable way of dealing with them – if you are reduced to head-scratching attempts to understand each new concept afresh. By contrast the regular sequence of looking for definitions, synonyms, universe, antonyms, antonyms of antonyms, partner words, and different forms of the concept can quickly, almost automatically create a wealth of information about any new or difficult idea. Above all, instead of having a single synonym or a skeletal definition of a term, by applying this checklist you should be able to generate a whole field of ideas relevant to your problem concept. Once you have such a field, narrow definitional questions tend to recede into the background, and questions about the relationships between different concepts become correspondingly more important.

3.2 RELATIONSHIPS BETWEEN CONCEPTS

Essay or exam questions quite commonly employ two or three problem concepts, which need to be clarified simultaneously if the question is to be tackled effectively. The words which create difficulties may not be simply the overtly academic terms, but also the ordinary language ideas used in conjunction with them. In the simplest situation, the essay question introduces two connected concepts.

Analysing Pairs of Concepts

Most people confronted by a pair of ideas used together seek for the simplest possible relationship, for example by dichotomizing them. False dichotomies occur where clearly separate terms are inappropriately overpolarized, i.e. treated not just as distinct but also as diametrically opposed. Another common reaction is to use two quite similar terms as if they effectively had the same meaning. Sometimes this usage is justified (for example, I have used 'ideas' and 'concepts' interchangeably throughout this chapter). But it is just as easy to exaggerate similarities between concepts as to overpolarize them. Where terms are clearly connected, yet distinct and complementary, the notion of 'a continuum' or 'a spectrum' ranging from one concept to the other is often introduced. The idea here is that two polar concepts are connected by some sort of single graduated scale with a number of intermediate positions. Applied to a false dichotomy (such as the democracy/totalitarianism contrast) this solution often yields some improvement. But it is actually quite rare to find that the meanings of different concepts can sensibly be ranged along a single dimension, for this presupposes some underlying common basis for comparison. Far more often the differences between concepts range along several dimensions at once (as in the democracy/totalitarianism contrast). Trying to reduce this differentiation to a single aspect of the terms' meanings usually sacrifices important information.

Yet Lewis (1974) points out that the relations between pairs of concepts can be exhaustively pictured with an analytical apparatus which is only slightly more complex. There are only four possible patterns of association or dissociation:

(i) **The two concepts** (A and B) **can be quite separate from each other**, with no overlap of meaning. In this

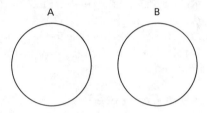

case there are only two distinct areas of reference to establish for the relationship to be completely understood. Complete separation implies that to know what one concept means is of little or no use to you in defining what the other concept means.

(ii) **They may overlap with each other**, implying the existence of an area of meaning or a class of objects to which both concepts apply. Here there are three areas which need to be established, A alone, B alone, and the

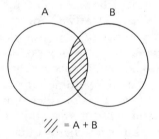

$\mathbin{/\!\!/} = A + B$

overlap area. Obviously the extent of the joint A + B area is critical in determining how similar the concepts are.

(iii) **One concept may wholly include the other**, in this case B is a subset or component of the higher order

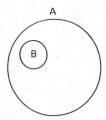

concept A. Determining this kind of relationship is much the trickiest of all the possible relations, since concept A may be quite appropriately applied in most or all of the contexts where B applies, implying that they can easily be seen as identical. However, the converse does not hold: there are areas of concept A where concept B cannot be appropriately used. The size of the A-only area is crucial in determining how similar the concepts are. It is also important to double-check which concept includes the other. Does A include B, or does B perhaps include A?

(iv) **The concepts may be completely identical**, so that there is only one area of meaning to be established.

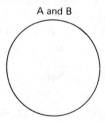

Visualizing More Complex Relationships

These simple patterns of association between ideas quickly become quite complex when more than two ideas have to be handled at once. It is rather rare for essay or exam questions to introduce more than two or three problem concepts to be handled simultaneously. But, of course, your own attempts to clarify concepts can multiply the number of ideas to be handled. A diagram or jotting is the best way to get a better grip on these more complex interrelationships between ideas. The main alternatives are as follows.

(a) **Venn diagrams** (such as Figures 3.1 and 3.2), which allow you to put together more intricate combinations of the four basic relationships discussed above. If you draw them large enough and write copious notes to yourself about what falls into the overlap areas between concepts, or which elements of a larger (more inclusive) idea are covered also by a more specific concept, then Venn diagrams need not become too intimidating.

(b) **A matrix of concept interconnections.** Here you simply write a list of the concepts you have to deal with along the top of a sheet of paper, and the same list down the left-hand side of the paper. Drawing vertical and horizontal lines between each item in the lists generates a grid. In each square you then write in the nature of the relationship between the two concepts (i.e. identity, inclusion, overlap or separation), adding whatever extra notes may be useful about the precise nature of the relationship.

Especially in the humanities many students have rarely encountered matrices and associate them vaguely with the mathematics they found difficult at school. In fact simple matrices are powerful tools for clarifying conceptual relationships and theoretical arguments. Consider Figure 3.3 which is a table with two columns and two rows showing how the arms race might develop. The USA (the column variable) and the USSR (the row variable) both have two options: to co-operate in the search for arms controls or to rearm unilaterally. Putting their options together creates four possible outcomes, shown by the boxes in the table. If both sides co-operate then arms control is assured, while if both sides refuse to negotiate a further escalation of the arms race is inevitable. If one side unilaterally restricts its rearmament the existing balance of power is upset, leaving it in an inferior military situation. Obviously you could add more rows and columns to handle extra options for each side, thereby rapidly increasing the number of possible outcomes. But even the simplest matrix of possibilities is illuminating because it reveals the basic structure of superpower relations. As in this case, the

	United States	
	Negotiate arms reductions	Build new generation of nuclear weapons
Soviet Union Negotiate arms reductions	Mutual force reductions	US military superiority
Build new generation of nuclear weapons	Soviet military superiority	New arms race

Figure 3.3: A matrix of nuclear options confronting the superpowers

main usefulness of matrices is that you must explicitly consider all the possible situations or relationships which are created when several 'variables' are combined. The table forces you to think through how to label each of the cells indicated.

(c) **Two-dimensional graphs** can be used instead of matrices where the row and column variables in a table are not just

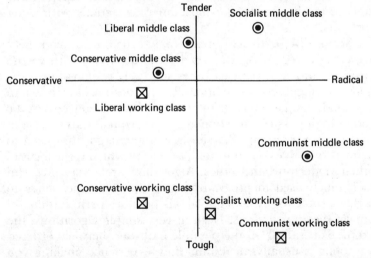

Figure 3.4: An example of a two-dimensional graph: Eysenck's map of the psychology of political attitudes
(The vertical scale shows how 'tough-minded' or 'tender-minded' people are; the horizontal scale shows how 'conservative' or 'radical' people are in their political beliefs.)
(From H. J. Eysenck, 'Primary Social Attitudes', in *British Journal of Sociology* 1951, p. 198; also *Sense and Nonsense in Psychology*, Penguin Books, 1957, p. 303.)

yes/no dichotomies, but continuous dimensions. Figure 3.4 shows an example used by the psychologist H. J. Eysenck. Here the horizontal dimension of the graph shows how left- or right-wing people are in their political views, and the vertical axis shows how 'tough' (= uncompromising) or 'tender' (= conciliatory) they are in expressing them. Whether you accept Eysenck's categories or not, the graph obviously presents a lot of ideas quickly, and allows a large number of political beliefs to be flexibly categorized.

(d) **'Tree' or 'string bag' diagrams** are constructed by drawing a circle or node for each idea in a system of ideas and then radiating lines between them to show interconnections. With tree diagrams (as with conventional notes) you have to work out the most basic (the root) idea in a network, and then rank other concepts below it like an organization chart for an army. With 'string bag' diagrams, however, you do not need to identify the major or most basic ideas at the start. Instead you simply build up the diagram as a network and the major ideas emerge as those with the most interconnections with other concepts.

(e) **Simple algorithms** (often loosely called 'flow diagrams') are constructed by organizing a set of questions with yes/no answers into a sequence. Lines for each response link the questions together. Conventionally the questions are drawn in diamond or square boxes, and the terminating concepts at the end of each possible question/response sequence are drawn in circular boxes. Figure 3.5 shows a simple algorithm used to define 'collective consumption', a concept which is the focus of much modern urban studies. Algorithms are a very powerful tool, much used in programming computers which have to tackle problems by looking at all possible permutations of binary (yes/no) options. Even in very simple algorithms, the exercise of tracing all the possible pathways between ordered questions is usually an illuminating experience, making you aware of possibilities you had never previously considered. Algorithms can display many different patterns of relationships between ideas.

The best kinds of visual representations are like those shown here, operating within some quite precise rules and bringing out the logical relationships between complex sets of concepts.

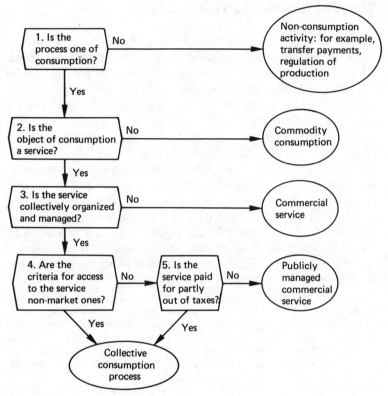

Figure 3.5: An example of a simple algorithm
(Dunleavy's criteria for determining whether a social process can be included within 'collective consumption'.)

Source: Dunleavy (1980, p. 53).

For social science students most of these devices should become familiar tools at some stage in your degree work. Visualizing interconnections between ideas is just as important in the humanities, but literary habits and traditional prohibitions in schools often create a prejudice against using diagrams in essays. However, these devices are primarily useful in clarifying your own thinking and note-taking, whether or not you include diagrams in your finished written work.

The Core Concepts in Your Discipline

All the disciplines in the humanities and social sciences have some central ideas and a certain body of technical knowledge which degree-level students must master. The more you appreciate the relationships between these core concepts, the more important it is to ask whether this material is building up into a cumulative picture – whether you are achieving a synthesis of what you have learnt. This cumulation of knowledge is not automatic, because the characteristic direction of modern academic development is towards increasing topic fragmentation. Course subjects get broken down into finer specialisms as research proceeds along separate avenues. Different vocabularies of concepts are developed for handling aspects of the same phenomena. In some areas technical methods develop rapidly, becoming more esoteric, while in other areas analysis remains more literary or intuitive in character:

> In this sense, there is a progressive splintering of the overall subject matter into more and more specialisms of a distinct kind. Unfortunately very few people ever try to collect up the specialisms in order to see how they can be assembled into an overall, systematized and well-related totality.
>
> There are grounds for believing that this lack of systematization is a source of great disappointment for students who are encountering the subject matter for the first time. All disciplines are characterized by a distinctive cluster of concepts and the beginning student naturally wants to know, quite early on, how these concepts hang together. However as he diligently reads more and more, and attends more and more lectures, he comes to realize that this key question (of how the key concepts hang together) is never going to be answered. What's more it does not matter that no answer is given, because the question is not going to be confronted anywhere in the final examination or assessment procedures! . . .
>
> In the field of social psychology, for example, there are almost no systematic attempts to inter-relate the notions of attitude, value, prejudice, disposition, habit, character trait and the like. [Again in sociology] textbooks there is very little which enables the student to distinguish between roles, rituals, statuses, duties, functions, and the like. . . . In the field of jurisprudence, we find similar confusions about the way in which laws, customs, conventions, rules, rituals, habits and the like, are inter-related. In the field of theology there likewise seems to be no agreement (and in many texts, not even a viewpoint) on the way in which the Christian conception of love (agape) is related to such notions as acceptance, self-sacrifice, respect, mutuality, friendship, eros, epithymia,

and so on ... [Across] the whole of the social and educational and behavioural sciences, and throughout the humanities as well, numerous examples of this kind can be found.

(Lewis, 1974, pp. 8, 10, 13)

The trouble with leaving your conceptual framework in this shape is that it is difficult for your own writing and thinking to be 'grounded': founded upon a systematic, internalized pattern of knowledge. Instead you are limited to using different bits and pieces of other peoples' ideas in different contexts. Even many lecturers operate with their knowledge organized in this way, as a collection of well-rehearsed formulae for different occasions, rather than as a systematized whole. But if this is true of people who spend their entire working lives in one discipline, why should students try to do any better?

Paradoxically, it is more important for students to ask questions about interconnections and relationships between concepts and topics. Academics can practise year in and year out on the subject material. Thus they quickly acquire a diffuse 'sense of occasion' which guides them in choosing which of a bunch of similar but differentiated concepts to use. Similarly they develop a knack for attuning their account of a topic to the prevailing academic style. In a way they have to think about how to say things less because they have just done it more often. But students spending no more than two terms or a year on any one course subject make mistakes much more frequently; they use a word or concept out of context, misapplying an idea or handling a topic in an inappropriate way.

Many students do feel that they achieve an overall orientation to their subjects – only very late in the day. Typically it is when you are revising for exams that fruitful interconnections and insights gell. But by this stage time is desperately limited. You cannot really follow up these insights, or use them to tackle any genuinely new material. So a practical aim is not to achieve some high-level redefinition of your subject which has eluded your teachers, but to try to acquire an overall 'feel' for its core concepts and the connections between topics early enough for it to be really useful in your academic work.

The key step is to ask questions of your source materials or teachers, such as: 'Concept A and concept B seem to be very similar. What precisely is the difference between them? Are there contexts where I should use one in preference to the other?' Pay attention to any source, especially a good textbook section, which explicitly examines the interrelationships between ideas or topics. Similarly when using a specialist subject dictionary, follow up cross-references to other entries. Since it is hard enough to make sense of individual topics and master the detail involved, it can be tempting to pass by interconnections and to slip easily into the established topic boundaries. If a question about interrelationships which has not been tackled in the lectures or reading does occur to you, it is also easy to assume that it is not an important point since it has not been dealt with explicitly. This is rarely the case. Most questions about interconnections are worth asking, even if the problem is as simple as the frequent cases of 'confuser' words, which sound the same (or sound as if they are related) but in fact have different meanings and derivations.

3.3 WHY CONCEPTS AND THEORIES ARE DISPUTED

There are three reasons why clarifying ideas in the humanities and social sciences is an especially difficult undertaking. First, the terminology of these disciplines often derives from everyday language and has to be connected to 'ordinary knowledge' to be intelligible. Second, all key academic concepts are integrated into profound theoretical disputes. Third, some key concepts may even be 'essentially contested', i.e. incapable of being given a single invariant meaning. All these features point up the importance of 'relational argument' in degree-level study.

Everyday Language and Academic Vocabularies

Unlike the physical sciences, the humanities and many social sciences do not have a separate sphere of 'scientific' discourse in which meanings are single-valued and unambiguous. On the contrary, they operate with central ideas taken from ordinary language. These 'everyday' terms almost invariably have more than one possible meaning. In ordinary conversation and other common usage, there are mechanisms for managing the flow of ideas with multiple meanings. The language being used often relates to an immediate context of experience. And personal interactions in a conversation can quickly correct mis-apprehensions or cases where people are inadvertently using identical words with different meanings. Translating the same terminology into an academic environment, and applying it to more abstract concerns, clearly opens up a potential for increased confusion. In many cases academic work has taken up and extended one or more of the multiple everyday meanings of ideas, producing an overlaying of academic and ordinary language senses of byzantine complexity. For example, one study counted 95 separate senses in which social scientists used the term 'community', many of them similar or overlapping, but others quite plainly contradictory (Hillery, 1955).

Faced with the need to conduct long exercises to retrieve an acceptable meaning of most of the currency of academic disputes, students can legitimately become impatient. It is easy to suspect that we are the victims of a previous 'artificial' debate by time-serving theoreticians justifying their existence by coining esoteric variants of meaning for established concepts. At least some of the time such a suspicion is well-founded. Academic disciplines have their fair share of 'arguments about nothing', with people talking past each other rather than appreciating different senses of the same ideas.

But most of the time there are good reasons why disputes over multiple meanings are perfectly serious and important areas of controversy. The key thing to appreciate here is the enormous social significance of language, especially where it refers to complex ideas reflecting fundamental human concerns. Terms and concepts with political, economic and social connotations can crystallize the ambitions, loves, hopes, fears, or loathings of classes, races, castes, parties, regions, or nations. Other psychological, anthropological and philosophical ideas define the possibilities which we have available to analyse and describe intensely-felt individual and interpersonal emotions:

Talk involves a competitive exchange of symbols, referential and emotive, through which values are shared and assigned and coexistence attained. . . . That talk is powerful is not due to any potency in words, but to needs and emotions in men. . . . A word or a phrase which has become established as connoting threat or reassurance for a group thus can become a cue for the release of energy out of all proportion to the apparent triviality of meaning suggested by its mere form. The word is not in itself the cause; but it can evoke everything about the group situation that lends emotion to its political interests, abstracting, reifying and magnifying.

(Edelman, 1963, pp. 114–16)

Academic discussions cannot be insulated from such basic human reactions and emotions. And the direct cross-over of concepts from everyday language to academic work carries with it powerful implications for the integration of these professional debates into wider social conflicts and controversies. As the scale of higher education has grown, so the scope of this integration has widened, until today the humanities and social sciences are key contributors to social debate around a wide range of personal, political, historical, economic and social questions.

A second central reason for 'crossovers' between academic and social debates is that the high-level knowledge produced by the humanities and social sciences is very restricted in scope. Academic work on the operations of social, political and economic systems or about human literature, culture, psychology and understandings may seem an impressive accumulation of authoritative material. But this kind of specialized, intense knowledge, the product of a frontal, rational analytic attack on problems, coexists with a radically different kind of 'ordinary' knowledge, often labelled 'common sense':

By 'ordinary knowledge' we mean knowledge that does not owe its origin, testing, degree of verification, truth status, or currency to distinctive [academic] professional techniques but rather to common sense, casual empiricism, or thoughtful speculation and analysis. . . . Everyone has ordinary knowledge – has it, uses it, offers it. It is not, however, a homogenous commodity. Some ordinary knowledge, most people would say, is more reliable, more probably true, than other.

(Lindblom and Cohen, 1979, p. 12)

Much academic work in the social sciences and humanities

simply produces more ordinary knowledge. For example, this book is almost completely ordinary knowledge. I hope that its recommendations are fairly plausible and reliable, but nonetheless they have no more authority or status than any other piece of common sense reasoning. Only very rarely is the tiny addition of knowledge from a single academic study independently useful or comprehensible. To see its significance we need to situate it within a closely specified context of existing knowledge, the vast bulk of which is ordinary knowledge. Hence the ideal of hermetically sealing off academic work from contact with everyday discourse, which has been seriously advocated from time to time by technocratic writers in several disciplines, is an illusion. In the humanities and social sciences, academic enterprise is parasitic upon a stock of ordinary knowledge which it can at best partially reformulate and supplement with superior status knowledge in some isolated and fragmented areas.

This inevitable integration can be managed fairly satisfactorily by existing academic defence mechanisms, to somewhat reduce the extent to which people in research and higher education respond automatically or emotively to verbal cues. But the price of creating an enlarged area of tolerant and rational discussion is constant vigilance over terms and ideas, especially where their meanings are disputed root and branch by different schools of thought.

Divergent Theoretical Approaches

The humanities and social sciences are inherently multi-theoretical. There is no single approach to any of these disciplines which commands a consensus within the academic community concerned. Instead there are multiple competing ways of 'doing' the subject.

(a) **'Political' world views** are perhaps the most obvious lines of disagreement. For example, there are conservative, Marxist or liberal approaches to topics as diverse as species change in biology, or the meaning of a Shakespearian text. In these macro-views academic work is often seen as part of a broader social 'project' – advancing the interests of a particular social class or group, promoting an ideal (for example, 'building socialism' or 'defending freedom'), and shaping the cultural climate of a whole society. Many 'political' affiliations are not to a formal political party; broader attachments to a social movement, religion, or way of life are just as important. In the humanities many literary and philosophical positions have been linked with more extensive cultural movements – such as modes of developing, interpreting and criticizing music, art, architecture, drama, or film. Existentialism in France or the work of the Frankfurt School in West Germany are good examples.

(b) Some **trans-disciplinary intellectual approaches** cut across subject areas and 'political' divisions. For example, 'structuralist' work in mathematics, educational psychology, linguistics, social theory and anthropology emphasizes 'systems of transformations' whose internal rules impersonally determine the future development of a set of phenomena (Piaget, 1972). In sociology some US structuralists are conservatives, but in West European social theory structuralism is extensively associated with Marxist thought (Blau and Merton, 1981). Similarly, sweeping claims for the compatability of a 'systems' perspective with the concerns of different disciplines or 'political' views have been influential (von Bertalanffey, 1968).

(c) **Method-based approaches** are medium-range influences based on particular styles or technologies of academic work. They are usually confined to groups of related subjects. For example, the procedures of mainstream economics have been extended into a general 'public choice' approach to political institutions, legal systems, trade unions, and so on. Across many social sciences the post-war development of computerized methods for analysing masses of data inaugurated a 'behavioural revolution' focusing on very quantitative approaches to mass behaviour and rejecting previous 'impressionistic' empirical work.

(d) **Epistemological disputes** are based on different approaches to the theory of knowledge (epistemology). For example, individualists view society and social institutions as straightforward products of individual actions, while holistic approaches regard them as complicated systems ('machines') with their own distinctive operations and real effects. Even in literature or philosophy we could explain a particular writer's works in terms of her life-history, personal experiences and predispositions; or interpret them instead as 'texts' encapsulating the broad social conflicts and ideologies of their period.

(e) **Subject-specific controversies** are more limited disagreements between schools of thought. Such disputes often arise between 'traditionalists' and 'revisionists' in a discipline; between different generations of academics; or between writers from countries, regions or centres of research with distinctive ways of proceeding. They can cover a bewildering range of questions – the appropriate methods for studying particular phenomena; the relative importance of different branches of the subject; the central questions which ought to be addressed; the criteria for deciding arguments' plausibility; and the validity of existing applied or empirical work. But in most subjects at any one point in time (certainly within a particular college) there will tend to be a more widely accepted 'mainstream' approach, and some kind of dissenting view.

All of these possible lines of dispute characteristically overlay each other in virtually every discipline. Theories, methods and evidence/analysis – none of these can be taken as 'settled', 'accepted' or resolved. Many of these disputes crystallize in fierce controversy over the concepts which form the building blocks of each discipline.

Essentially Contested Concepts

There are many circumstances where people can share a concept, agreeing that it applies in some cases, but in other situations disagreeing whether it applies or not. For example, there may be a substantial measure of agreement that a wide range of artefacts qualify as 'works of art', but simultaneously fierce disputes about whether other pieces of work should be labelled in the same way. These debates are not about empirical questions, but arise because considerations of vital importance to one school of thought in assessing 'works of art' are seen as marginal by others.

These conceptual disputes may be irresolvable where:

(i) **the concept is appraisive**, describing a generally valued ideal or situation;

(ii) **it is a complex, multi-dimensional concept**, with room for disagreement about how to weight different elements; and

(iii) **the language rules governing how to use the term are relatively open**, so that there is scope for dispute about whether the concept applies to subjects which are novel, unanticipated or qualitatively different from past applications.

If all three conditions are met then Gallie (1959) considered that the concept could be described as essentially contested.

A hallmark of essentially contested concepts is that disputes about meanings and applications are bound to be endless, cycling back and forth with no possibility of reaching agreement between different approaches. In Gallie's view, this diversity is not just inevitable and acceptable, but valuable. The recognition of partially shared and partially distinct usages enriches thought and language amongst all participants. Ideas such as 'liberty', 'progress', 'health', 'democracy', 'beauty', 'fashion', 'love', 'true religion', 'Christian doctrine', 'justice', and so on, touch upon disputes of fundamental significance for the human condition.

> Since we often cannot expect knockdown arguments to settle these matters, we must come to terms somehow with the political [or ethical or ideological] dimensions of such [conceptual] contests. It is possible, and I believe likely, that the politics of these contests would become more enlightened if the contestants realized that in many contexts no single use can be advanced that must be accepted by all reasonable persons. The realization that opposing uses might not be exclusively self-serving but have defensible reasons in their support could introduce into these contests a measure of tolerance and a receptivity to reconsideration of received views. . . . These conclusions are themselves disputable. They flow from the assumption that rationality, fragile as it is, is helped, not hindered, by heightened awareness of the nature and import of our differences.
>
> (Connolly, 1974, p. 40)

Hence it is important to pay special attention to disputes over ideas or terms with a strong normative function, particularly where they relate to central human or social values which are internally complex and need extensive interpretation before being applied to specific situations. The possibility of a concept being 'essentially contested' should not become a cop-out option to be applied in any hard-to-resolve dispute over meanings. Indeed the existence of this class of concepts is itself the subject of fierce controversy. But so long as Gallie's three conditions are met, taking the prospect seriously may greatly illuminate some long-running controversies in the humanities and social sciences.

The Importance of Relational Argument

Education in the humanities and less technical social sciences is frequently justified in terms of developing in students the ability to analyse problems non-dogmatically – rationally weighing the pros and cons of a preferred approach against the claims of alternative interpretations. However, many people entering higher education find it perplexing that there is no unanimity, but instead deeply felt division amongst their teachers and source materials on how to tackle problems. Contemporary popular images of the physical sciences as built around universally accepted and well-verified laws about the natural world, have created similar expectations about the humanities and social sciences. Hence the sorts of knowledge actually offered by these multi-theoretical disciplines can easily seem primitive, half-formed, or as yet inadequately developed.

Many people come to college with fixed attitudes and a belief that there is 'one best way' of tackling issues in their subject (Perry, 1968). Confronted with evidence of divergent approaches they initially feel that one of the groups of academics involved must be correct, and the other group wrong-headed or incompetent. A more sophisticated suspicion among students is that their teachers are exposing them to divergent approaches to keep the course discussion sessions going when the issues could be fairly simply resolved. Or perhaps lecturers want some students to commit themselves to a wrong approach, which can be corrected, creating pedagogical gains for the class as a whole. As chronic exposure to competing views makes these Machiavellian interpretations seem less plausible, many students lapse into complete relativism – arguing that all viewpoints are as good as any other, it all depends what your starting point is or which values you identify with. Only a minority of people develop a stage further, making a reasoned, conditional commitment to one approach while acknowledging the existence of alternative viewpoints.

Not all college courses are explicitly orientated towards developing relational knowledge. Sometimes divergent approaches are treated within one degree but in separate courses, each of which is taught in a monothematic way. Control over courses is an important way in which academics in different schools of thought advance their position inside their department, and more broadly in their profession. Undeniably there are some trade-offs between developing specialized knowledge and skills on a course and considering a variety of perspectives. But any decently run course should give some explicit attention to possible criticisms of the approach being followed.

Where a course is a jealously guarded preserve of teachers committed to a single approach, students sometimes wonder seriously about the advisability of adopting a different perspective. Such a situation negates the fundamental purposes of higher education. The teachers concerned often rationalize their stance by claiming that they are not penalizing unorthodox views so much as registering disquiet with their crude expression. However, it is the decision to teach courses in a single-track approach which deprives students of the help of reading lists and tutorial guidance, and crucially limits their abilities to express alternative views at the right level.

Where courses are taught from an explicitly multi-theoretical perspective, relational thinking can still be hindered because alternative perspectives are considered on different topics. If topics are handled in discrete packages, each with their own set of concepts and controversies (pp. 64–6), making connections from one to another is difficult and people get 'locked into' using each approach only on separate issues.

Summary of Suggestions: Analysing Concepts and Theories

1. Be aware that direct methods of understanding meanings, such as definitions or synonym-hunting, may be overprecise, hence sacrificing valuable information (p. 49).

2. Use indirect as well as direct methods to understand problem terms. Look for the concept's universe, antonyms, antonyms of antonyms, unstated partner words, and different forms of the concept (p. 51).

3. Beware of false dichotomies. Search for the most inclusive possible antonym, whose antonym in turn leads back to the original concept (p. 52).

4. Watch for unstated partner words, which can inflate the scope of disputes unnecessarily (p. 55).

5. If a question asks about a concept in one form, your response will usually involve using its other forms – so be clear how to use these terms as well (p. 55).

6. Analyse the relation between pairs of concepts using the categories of separation, overlap, inclusion, and identity (p. 58).

7. Try to visualize more complex relations between concepts – for example, using Venn diagrams, matrices, two-dimensional graphs, 'tree' and 'string bag' diagrams, or simple algorithms (p. 60).

8. Use jottings and diagrams to clarify your own thinking, even if you will not include them in your finished writing (p. 63).

9. Try to understand how the core concepts in your discipline relate to each other. Ask questions about how concepts and topics interconnect, even if they are normally handled in a very fragmented fashion (p. 65).

10. Recognizing the interconnections between academic vocabularies and everyday language, and between academic inquiry and 'ordinary knowledge', will help you understand the importance of disputes about meaning (p. 66).

11. To understand the argumentative disputes in your area, ask whether they involve: 'political' world views; trans-disciplinary approaches; method-based approaches; epistemological disputes; or subject-specific controversies (p. 69).

12. Where a concept is appraisive, multi-dimensional, and has open language rules governing its use, take seriously the possibility that it may be 'essentially contested' (p. 72).

13. Recognize the importance of relational argument in the humanities and social sciences (p. 73).

The problem: cut a hole in a postcard big enough to put your head through:

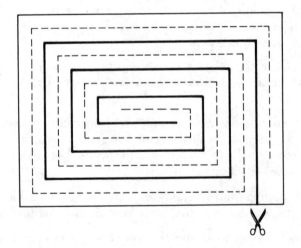

One solution
Cut the postcard in the helix shape shown by the solid black line. Then make a slit up the middle of the helix-shaped strip as shown by the dotted black line, taking care to leave some uncut paper at each end

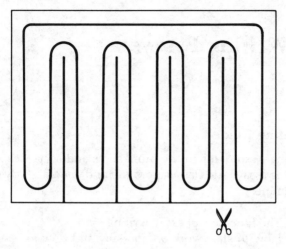

Another solution
Make the cuts shown by the solid black lines

Two possible solutions to de Bono's 'lateral thinking' puzzle. For a full discussion of this puzzle, see E. de Bono, *The Mechanism of Mind* (Harmondsworth, Penguin, 1971), pp. 172–6.

4 Writing Essays

Reading Guide

For many students in the humanities and social sciences, writing essays and class papers is a fundamental study skill. I examine:

1. The functions of essay writing.
2. How to start work on an essay and how to respond effectively to a question.
3. Some basic approaches to structuring essays, and their advantages and disadvantages.
4. How to plan essays and use 'organizers' in the text.
5. Style and composition questions.

4.1 THE FUNCTIONS OF ESSAY WRITING

Writing essays and papers is an essential step in promoting intellectual development, internalizing knowledge (pp. 3–5) and developing the capacity for relational argument (pp. 73–4). These objectives may seem rather grand and remote when applied to your own essay writing. Yet they are the most important rationale of universities' and polytechnics' stress upon individual written work. It is not that lecturers like reading précis of familiar textbooks, drastically abbreviated and with additional spelling mistakes. Rather, despite years of effort to diversify methods of higher education, there still is no better way of fostering intellectual development in many subjects than requiring students to produce (and then defend and discuss) essays which crystallize their own understanding of the coursework. In addition essay writing has two more immediate functions.

Generating Feedback

One of the things which distinguishes studying for a degree from lower level coursework is that many people experience a sudden reduction in feedback about how they are getting on. In schools or further education colleges teachers usually set marked pieces of work to class groups every other week. Hence school sixth formers know where they stand within their peer group very accurately. But at university or polytechnic students may complete only two or three essays per subject in a term, which are individually marked and discussed with a tutor or class teacher. Hence students can find it hard to judge whether they are doing well or badly by comparison with their year group. Sometimes tutors take a keen interest in students' overall development across all the subjects they are studying; but only sometimes.

Amongst students who worry about performing badly on a course, essay writing is one of the first activities to slip. They develop 'a block' about revealing their non-progress to anyone. While they assiduously attend lectures (perhaps the next one will make sense) and turn up to classes (but say nothing), their written work gets more and more infrequent. This is a vicious spiral where people become cut off from any genuine awareness of how they are doing, and from useful advice. Class teachers and tutors need to look at individual written work before they can tell how someone is coping with a subject, where their difficulties and strengths may lie, and what kinds of things they should try to do differently. A short essay is a much better basis from which to offer helpful advice than observing someone's class participation (which may be minimal anyway for personality reasons).

Sometimes students are put off handing in essays because class teachers and tutors keep a record of their marks on written work. But unless there is a continuous assessment system, individual essay marks do not count towards your class of degree. They are kept mainly as a safeguard should you fall ill during the exams, and so on. At times, teachers' feedback will be critical, albeit in a constructive way. But at other times it will be encouraging and supportive, confirming your advances, promoting your self-confidence and pinpointing avenues for further development. In order to generate feedback observe the following points.

Write early and often – do not postpone your first essay until the end of term while you get the hang of the subject. Write at least one or two in the first half of term and do not be too mortified to find you still have a long way to go. Similarly do not write one 'perfect' essay in place of a number of attempts at different topics. In any course where you have to sit exams, you will need to cover a spread of topics; so having one or two overly crafted essays is no good to you.

Write in your own way – essays can only generate a useful response from teachers if what they read reflects your own understanding of the subject expressed in your own words. 'Cribbing' parts of an essay (unacknowledged quotation) is pointless – for then the feedback you obtain is based on someone else's thinking. This might persuade a class teacher that you are doing more work in a subject than you are in practice. But it does not help you to appreciate how well you are doing or what to do to improve your performance.

In addition, because your essays should be responses to specific questions asked in class reading lists (or previous exams), 'lifting' material or 'rewriting the textbook' almost always creates problems of irrelevance. In the social sciences and humanities you will rarely find any one book or paper which tackles an essay topic in precisely the same way that you have been asked. Because your source materials are written with other concerns in mind, there will be a perceptible lack of fit between them and the essay question. The less you reprocess information yourself, the more likely it is that you are talking off the point. Hence good essay writing always involves you in *adapting* material produced for one purpose to fit a different question.

Write essays to elicit improvements – not to be confirmed in your own high opinion of your work. Everyone identifies with their own written work – academics and students more than most. It is very natural given the mental effort and physical slog you have committed to an essay, to fall into a defensive posture when criticisms are made of it – to code the criticisms as hostile, unhelpful or unreasonable. But however biased or pre-judged any criticism may be it is rarely without some value for you. Even the most destructive critic has to have weak points in your argument to latch on to, gaps to point out, or misunderstandings to correct. And these are exactly the items you need to discover.

Finally, **be persistent in seeking information** – do not be put off if an essay you have submitted does not reappear quickly, or if it comes back with only a few words of enigmatic scrawl at the end. Class teachers and tutors are very human. They can mislay essays (so keep your originals and give them a photocopy); and they may mark your essays in a hurry (so they should be able to expand on cryptic comments if asked). Even with more extended feedback, if you cannot follow a criticism or do not understand a grade, always make sure you ask for clarification.

Preparing for Assessment

In many courses part of the assessment takes the form of essays submitted for marking. Often these essays are the best of a larger number of assignments completed during the course; alternatively, they may be considered responses to specially set questions handed out at the end of the year. In this situation normal essay writing provides a direct preparation for at least part of your assessment. Even where the coursework to be handed in is a much longer dissertation, essay writing is a key activity for picking a topic and developing the appropriate authoring skills (Chapter 5).

But for most students, examinations continue to play a major role in their assessment. Many people worry a great deal about examinations, and orientate everything they do during a year's work towards them. Others prefer to concentrate on developing their thinking during the year in whatever way seems best, and focus on the examination only in the last few weeks. Teachers are similarly divided in their views. Some will stress that you should write short, timed essays from the word 'go'. Others argue that it is intellectually crippling to let exams become a straitjacket for your work; you need to be free to stretch your mental faculties and to develop high-quality writing powers in an individual style. There are pros and cons in both viewpoints and perhaps the best advice is to steer a middle course between them. Do not ignore the fact that your work will have to be focused within an examination type of assessment. But do not become obsessed by it either. Most exams require that you develop skills in answering questions, in rigorously selecting material to include in your answers, and in planning or organizing your work (Chapter 6). Each of these are skills you can develop a great deal in your essays and class papers, especially if you bear in mind the following points.

Always write essays in response to questions – never just write around a general theme or vague title. Writing answers to questions set by teachers gives you practice in analysing questions and maintaining a relevant response. It also allows teachers to give you advice on your approach. Ignoring the question asked, simply writing down everything you know about a topic, or writing about something completely different, are all ways of depriving yourself of this training and associated feedback. Occasionally you may be assigned only a general topic to tackle; in these cases always define a precise question of your own to which your essay is a response.

Write short essays, not long ones – an essay is what it says, literally 'an attempt' at tackling a subject. Ideally, an essay should be long enough for you to include relevant information, to synthesize a complex literature, to describe elaborate chains of events or ideas, and to express your own arguments properly. But it should not be so long that you are writing a mini textbook, or that the necessity for drastic simplification and selection of information is eased. Above all it should not be so long that you could not conceivably adapt the argument for use later under exam conditions (Chapter 6). Very long tutorial or class essays, worked over for weeks, where you can include absolutely everything you want to say, simply prevent you facing up to the difficulties of judging what material to put in and what to leave out. If you never practise this during the year, do not be surprised to find that you suddenly feel overloaded (not knowing where to start or what to include) in the examination itself.

Write essays fairly quickly – taking no more than a week in preparing a class paper or tutorial essay. In most exams you will typically only have 40 to 60 minutes per answer. Consequently one skill you need to practise during the year is how to speedily select the really useful material for inclusion. This knack is not just relevant for examinations. It is a key life skill in most career contexts (Chapter 7).

4.2 UNDERSTANDING ESSAY TOPICS

Getting down to writing an essay is a complex business. You need to track down some of the books on the reading list and digest them (Chapter 2). When a sufficiently impressive information base has been assembled – or perhaps more commonly when the possibilities of finding any more relevant information are exhausted – attention shifts to understanding the question and defining a response. Most students have the importance of writing 'relevant' answers dinned into them during their schooldays. So almost everyone will stare at the question for some period at this stage. Indeed, it is quite easy to be so preoccupied with relevance that you become hypnotized by the question set. A good indication of when you might be falling into this trance-like state is if you find yourself picking up phrases from the question and repeating them in your essay. Some people ritually incant a key phrase at the beginning or end of paragraphs to demonstrate that they are 'answering the question'. For example, if a topic asks whether Louis XIV was a figurehead or a driving force in the growth of absolute monarchies in seventeenth-century Europe, this phrase is likely to reappear in sentences such as 'Thus we can see that Louis XIV was indeed a driving force in the rise of absolutism', or vice versa. In practice, reiteration of the question wording usually indicates not a real concern for relevance but a failure to analyse the question and to translate it effectively into your own words. The whole chunks of wording being repeated are often precisely the elements of the question which have not been analysed at all.

There are several ways to improve how you analyse essay questions.

(a) Use techniques for analysing concepts contained in the

question. Generating a whole field of ideas around major concepts, and looking at the interrelationships between them (pp. 47–64), can provide a working basis for the whole essay-writing period. For major concepts this stage should obviously include definitions, synonyms, antonyms, antonyms of antonyms, partner words, different forms of the concept, and so on. But frequently it is the ordinary language words surrounding the specialized concepts which impart the distinctive slant to questions. A useful procedure is to work through every individual word in the essay question checking on its meaning in a dictionary (which will usually generate synonyms), and looking also for antonyms. For example, take the question: 'To what extent should ministers be able to control their civil servants?' The key word here is 'should', which means that the question is a normative one, about what *ought* to happen, not the much more commonly asked descriptive question, about what *does in practice* happen. When this question was used in an LSE first-year politics exam, around 80 per cent of those answering failed to notice the 'should', instead reproducing purely descriptive material about minister/civil service relations.

(b) **'Brainstorm' around the essay topic for a short period.** Brainstorming is a technique much used in management training and problem-solving. The idea is to respond to the essay question by spending a quarter of an hour writing down everything that comes into your head which might be relevant. Brainstorming is a period when you are deliberately *not* being critical of your own ideas, when you are trying to relax the mental barriers which normally inhibit lateral thinking. The idea is to break out of established patterns of thought, becoming aware of all kinds of mental cues which we may normally suppress. For example, try free associating ideas, saying a term aloud and seeing what other terms it suggests to you. The rationale behind brainstorming is that even if you analyse all the terms used in a question, you may do so with an overdefined initial idea of what the question means in the back of your mind. Relaxing this straitjacket for a period can often let stray thoughts surface which are important and possibly more original, helping to further enlarge the field of ideas which you consider in defining an answer. Of course, at the end of the

topic definition period you will need to go through your
brainstorming list removing any irrelevant ideas to avoid their
being incorporated into the essay answer itself. But at the stage
of understanding the topic you can afford to be a bit more
relaxed and adventurous in your thinking.

(c) **Translate the whole question into your own words.**
Frequently essay questions are extremely condensed,
especially if they are taken from past examination papers. In
translating the question into your own words, you should try to
unpack its meaning. If the original question took two lines, it
may be quite common for your translation to take five or six
lines. Try to avoid using any of the same wording as the
question. Translate specialized academic concepts into
ordinary language if possible. Translate also any significant
linking words into synonyms (possibly several synonyms).

(d) **Try writing down the opposite of the question.** Some
kinds of question can be illuminated by re-expressing them in a
reversed or negative form. For example, take the question
above on 'To what extent should ministers be able to control
their civil servants?' It can be hard to see what is problematic
here. The question wording directs our attention directly to the
democratic theory that elected politicians should determine
policy and that government officials should simply provide
advice for and implement these decisions. Hence the
temptation may be to give an 'unbalanced' answer, weighted
towards the primacy of ministerial control. But suppose we
alter the question to read: 'To what extent should ministers *not*
be able to control their civil servants?' Now a whole series of
different factors may come to mind. For instance, we probably
would not want ministers to be able to enforce law-breaking on
their officials, or lying to Parliament, or falsification of
government statistics. So reversing the question wording has
illuminated an area of legitimate civil service autonomy from
political influences which might otherwise have remained
latent.

(e) **Make sure you recognize open-ended questions.**
Particularly where an essay topic concerns the causes or origins
of an event or situation, it is common to find questions phrased
in the form: ' "The dominant influence on event X was cause
A". Discuss'. For example, a quotation might suggest that

Henry VIII's marital difficulties were the primary reason for the separation of the Church in England from Roman Catholicism. The question is open-ended because one possible line of reply would be to disagree with the quotation by saying that cause A was by no means the only factor involved in event X; causes B, C, D, E etc., all played an important role. Tempting though it may be, this line of attack actually moves away from the focus of the question (which is the role of cause A in event X), and on to a whole range of topics which have not been asked about (i.e. causes B, C, D, and E). If you are not careful, the essay becomes simply a catalogue of factors other than cause A, and loses a manageable focus of concerns. So once an open-ended question has been identified, you must formulate an explicit rationale for delimiting a manageable area of discussion. So long as you explain your decision somewhere in the essay, this self-conscious restriction of its focus is entirely legitimate.

4.3 TYPES OF ESSAY

Although each individual essay is unique, there are only a small number of *strategies* of essay writing. If you know what these basic ways of proceeding are, and their advantages or pitfalls, then you may find it easier to analyse your own approach and to plan essays more effectively in the future. There are three basic types of essay: descriptive, analytic, and argumentative.

Descriptive Essays

To write a descriptive essay you organize your material in the same way that the 'real world' is arranged. The structure of your essay is not something you work out for yourself but instead follows an externally given sequence. The most common kinds of descriptive essays include the following.

(a) **Chronological essays.** Here your response is organized around the development of a chain of events in time – as in treating historical events, focusing on the biographical development of a particular actor, discussing the evolution of an author's thought during his lifetime, or analysing the intellectual history of a stream of academic thought. The sequence in which events took place forms the main element of the essay's structure. This effect is particularly pronounced because most books covering this sort of topic organize their material chronologically. Narrative essays are slightly different in that they are structured not by a sequencing of events in real time but by the story-line of a novel, piece of drama, film, and so on. The essay has a descriptive structure because it replicates the narrative organization of the literature being subjected to critical attention.

Narrative and chronological essays always appear simple, since the question of how to organize material resolves itself into a 'natural' pattern with a beginning, middle and end. In practice, choosing a starting point from which to begin a chronological essay is often quite difficult. For example, most essay questions in history ask in an open-ended way about the origins or causes of particular events, specifying a concluding destination for the essay but not where to begin. Defining too early a starting point lengthens the essay and introduces material of attenuated relevance. Choosing a vague or variable starting point across different aspects of an essay question may create difficulties in arranging the material into a single narrative line. Yet in many essays the relevant time periods will be different across, say, political, religious or economic aspects of a problem. Normally chronological essays are best organized from some very precise starting point: the end of a previous era, a revolution or fundamental change of ideas, the accession of a new monarch, government or regime. As with all decisions about choosing periods, an explicit rationale for a particular starting point or claimed natural 'break' in the development of events always needs to be given.

(b) **The 'guidebook' pattern.** Here the essay follows some easy or obvious 'shopping list' of features drawn from the area of social life being discussed. Guidebook essays are as frequent a phenomenon in the social sciences as are chronologies in history or narrative essays in literature studies. For example, an essay in social policy or social administration dealing with how children are taken into care by local authorities might follow a guidebook pattern by discussing different categories of care specified in legislation. An essay in political science or applied economics which provides a tour round particular sets of institutions similarly fits the guidebook mould.

(c) **Random author sequence.** In this pattern the paragraph structure of the essay is provided by accounts of different authors whom the student has encountered in reading around the topic. Frequently an author's name is the very first word in each new paragraph; 'Jones argues that . . .', followed by a quick précis of Jones's account. For this sort of essay to remain descriptive (as distinct from argumentative essays considered below) two things are necessary. First, none of the author's positions are labelled. Each author's thought is treated as completely individual (almost idiosyncratic). There is no process of standing back and asking what kind of position it is that Jones is taking, no attempt to classify Jones in terms of some wider framework of theoretical or empirical controversy. Second, there is no discernible rationale or pattern about the sequence in which author views are presented. Different writers are summarized in a random sequence, as a bundle or collection with no internal organization. Often they are treated in the order that they were initially read and incorporated into a student's notes. Hence this pattern of essay writing remains descriptive, because the organizing framework for the essay is not thought through by the essay writer but created by the external literature.

Descriptive essays are usually the type favoured by beginning students and those who feel themselves less competent in doing a subject. The main reason for this predisposition is that with a descriptive approach you do not have to think too hard about how to plan the essay. The sequence of topics is already there in the material you are reading, and you need only to reproduce it. Begin at the beginning, go on until you come to the end, then stop. Not only is this the easy option intellectually, but much of the literature you are using will be written in a basically descriptive way. A further reason why so many people write descriptive essays is that this is the way they previously operated at school or college. Most education below degree level places a premium on factual knowledge, perhaps derived from reading a single textbook or at any rate a very restricted number of literature sources.

Descriptive essays are actually very hard to write well at degree level in the humanities and social sciences for three reasons. First, this pattern of organization requires a lot of applied or empirical material if the argument is to reach a reasonably high level. A chronological or guidebook structure can work tolerably well if you are writing a 200-page book, simply because you have space enough to cram in a mass of factual detail. But a descriptive structure is useless if you want to write a lively six page essay, which summarizes key issues without running through overly basic material. The essay organization does not suggest any rationale for selecting some areas for analysis and neglecting others. Instead it places a premium on comprehensiveness, on ordering material into a single chronological sequence, or describing all the relevant pieces of legislation, institutions, and so on.

Second, if they stay short, descriptive essays usually oversimplify complex narratives or organizational arrangements. The amount of detail required can be cut down only by giving a crude account of the subject. If they get longer descriptive essays can incorporate more empirical detail ('facts'), but only at the risk of losing a recognizable argument, and ceasing to be well-composed essays at all. Third, since there are very rarely subjects covered by just one textbook at degree level, even lengthy descriptive essays can look disorganized as the writer struggles to combine material drawn from differently structured sources. This is characteristically the point at which essays degenerate into a random sequence of authors' views. Overall, descriptive essays are best avoided if at all possible. They do not help you to select the material most useful for a short essay. They rarely look well planned or tightly argued.

Analytic Essays

There is no great secret involved in moving to a better pattern of essay organization. To write an analytic essay the subject matter is divided up into a number of categories you yourself define. Paragraphs are matched up with these categories, so that the essay is structured around them. Thus to some extent the essay material is transformed and reshaped in line with your personal mental framework. The categories used obviously depend on the topic being covered. But some widely used types of analytic essay include the following.

(a) **Periodized chronologies** – where real time is divided up into analytically defined periods. This is the quickest way to transform a question about a chain of events. Periodization helps to break away from the chronological form because the essay is no longer organized just around a dominant narrative line, dictated by the sequence in which external events occurred. Instead subject matter is split up into a small number of periods (for example, 'early', 'middle' and 'late'). But *within* each period the presentation of information can be reorganized. Those events or features which especially characterize each period can be selected and discussed in detail, without having to be presented in a chronological sequence. Developments which are identified analytically as less important or incidental to the progression from one period to the next can be excluded from discussion. Because each period is analysed as a whole, in a systematic (non-narrative) way, the essay can jump around in terms of references to historical time within each period, organizing discussion by reference to criteria other than temporal sequencing. Usually this makes it much easier to arrange material in a way which brings out themes and arguments clearly.

(b) **Systematic essays** operate by dividing up an integrated social process into component parts or subtopics. For example, an overall pattern of historical change could be discussed in terms of the economic, social, political and religious developments in a country. Each aspect is handled in a separate paragraph (or group of paragraphs) and the historical sequencing of events is subsumed into a general analytic discussion. The subtopics used in systematic essays naturally vary a great deal from one subject to another, and even within subjects from one question to another. The essence of systematic essay writing remains, however, the mental division of subject matter into categories formulated by the author, rather than taking these from the material itself.

(c) **Causal essays** tackle questions about the origins and patterns of causation of phenomena. They work by dividing up their subject matter, not into separate subtopics, but into 'causes' and 'effects', 'short-term' *vs* 'long-term' factors, 'structural' *vs* 'accidental' influences, or processes internal to a system *vs* external influences. In other words, the organizing framework for the essay is provided by explanatory categories generated by a causal account of situations or developments. Since a great many essay and exam questions in the humanities and social sciences focus on causation, essays organized in this way are very common.

Many students run into problems in causal essays because of the difficulty of handling 'multiple causation'. This label denotes a situation where there is no single overriding 'cause' of a phenomenon, but rather a whole variety of influences integrally involved in producing it. One quite effective way to organize thinking around this sort of problem is to bear in mind the distinction between a *sufficient cause* (where the occurrence of event A alone is enough to produce event B), and a *necessary* but not sufficient *cause* (where event A is a prerequisite for event B, but where A alone could not produce B). There may be many necessary conditions of an event or situation, but only one sufficient condition. In organizing a causal essay it obviously makes sense to decide at the outset whether there is any sufficient condition for an event or situation to occur, and if not how the remaining necessary conditions might be ranked in importance.

The advantages of an analytic structure over a descriptive pattern are threefold. First, you have more clearly mastered the subject, being able to organize discussion of the essay topic in a distinctively personal way. The essay paragraphs are clearly structured around your own mental constructs rather than externally given categories. To this extent an analytic structure will be much more useful in helping you to internalize knowledge, because to write it you must first transform the material more extensively than with a descriptive essay. Second, analytic essays usually look well-organized, as long as you signpost what you are doing for readers at the beginning (pp. 101–2), stick to your sequence of paragraphs, and choose robust categories that do not involve you in repeating material or saying nearly the same thing in different ways. Finally, a good analytic essay structure allows you to get to the heart of a topic or problem quickly, to avoid becoming involved in basic descriptions you can legitimately take as read, and to select only the most important material on which to concentrate attention. Whereas descriptive essays often seem to entail 'rewriting the textbook', analytic essays help your writing to start off at the right level (pp. 146–7).

The main disadvantages of analytic essays are common authoring difficulties. In dividing up the subject material you need to be sure that the categories chosen for different paragraphs do not overlap, and that similar background or narrative description will not recur at several different points in the argument. It is also important to arrange the categories being used into a pattern which is logical and builds up the essay argument in a cumulative fashion. An analytic essay structure can also mean that you have more difficulty in explaining theoretical differences or divergent empirical viewpoints than is the case with the last type of essay.

Argumentative Essays

The importance of relational argument in the humanities and social sciences has already been discussed (pp. 73–4). Neither descriptive nor analytic essay structures recognize this importance directly. Both patterns of organization tend to skew essay writing towards blandness – suppressing controversy in a bid to get a single coherent interpretation of a topic. Where the subject is actually the focus of considerable dispute, however, trying to manufacture a consensus view may appear instead as bogus, or as a slanted, monothematic exposition of one viewpoint. In particular, descriptive essays often present a lowest-common-denominator kind of view.

By contrast, in an argumentative essay the whole structure of paragraphs revolves around two or more competing perspectives on a topic. The essay sets out to elucidate their strengths, weaknesses and differences, and to decide which (if any) seems the most plausible. The viewpoints discussed may operate at many levels, ranging from sweeping intellectual perspectives spanning several disciplines to empirical controversies restricted to a single topic. Perhaps the easiest way to generate an argumentative pattern of organization is to ask what pro and anti views there could be on the essay topic. Where the essay question itself asserts a particular point of view, these positions may seem clear cut – do you agree or disagree with the view embodied in the question? But it is always worth asking whether things are as simple as that. For example, is it possible to disagree with the question from two different (even diametrically opposed) positions? Is there a viewpoint which would claim that the question itself is misformulated, biased or trivial? If the essay question appears rather anodyne or non-controversial, then the problem may be how to construct any decent argument around the topic. But remember: there are scarcely any areas of the humanities or social sciences where everyone agrees. Competing inter-pretations of a topic are the norm. If you cannot identify an area of controversy, perhaps you have not yet fully understood the topic?

The advantages of argumentative essays are threefold. First, they make the necessity for relational argument explicit in your essay organization. Second, they focus attention on the most controversial aspects of a topic, selecting material which is in dispute but allowing you to bypass arguments accepted by all viewpoints. Concentrating on alternative views can be an easy way of excluding very basic or descriptive material. Third, argumentative essays usually look well-organized, so long as your identification of viewpoints or perspectives is accurate, and you have a fair idea of which positions to describe.

Argumentative essays also have a number of disadvantages. It is typically quite hard to come to grips with broad theoretical differences between viewpoints early on in studying a subject. So you may be well advised to try writing analytic essays near the start of a course. Analytic essays fragment complex topics into more easily managed and understood individual aspects, whereas argumentative essays place a premium on understanding the topic as a whole. Argumentative essays also involve you in making more interconnections between different components of your studying – for example, between the reading you have done specifically for the essay topic, the discussions of previous topics in class, and a general course of lectures. So argumentative essays are harder to do if you are particularly concerned to 'catch up' on earlier neglect of a subject.

There are also a number of steps to take care over in composing argumentative essays.

(a) **Labelling viewpoints appropriately** is vital. Labels are key shortcuts to understanding a subject, summing up a whole collection of distinctive features quickly in two or three words (Chapter 3). Usually labels are partly descriptive, i.e. the term applied actually says something informative about the viewpoint. Hence it is rarely useful to structure an argumentative essay simply around disagreements between individual authors. Obviously proper names are useful if these authors are very major figures – such as founders of whole schools of analysis, for example, Marx, Weber, Freud or Keynes – or are major literary or philosophical figures whose works form a distinct oeuvre. But if they are contemporary commentators, it is relatively uninformative to know that 'Smith thinks this but Jones thinks that'. It is always worth standing back from the details of a writer's individual position and asking which school of thought or style of analysis (which '-ism') it is that she stands for. Even if the answer is that two authors speak from within the same '-ism' this is a useful piece of information if it stimulates you to ask what people from outside that '-ism' say about the subject. Above all, accurate and carefully considered labelling of viewpoints is essential if you are to ensure that an argumentative essay remains properly organized, and does not degenerate into the descriptive essay pattern where individual authors are surveyed in a random sequence. Labelling groups similar authors together and helps to clarify a logical sequence in which to consider a variety of viewpoints.

(b) **Presenting your own and other people's viewpoints** within the same essay requires careful management. I noted above the difficulties that you may face in adopting a personal position (pp. 73–4). At one pole are students trained at school to 'always put an argument' who pursue a single theme relentlessly, often against logic or the evidence. At another pole are people who find it inconceivable that anyone should be interested in their personal view when so many 'better qualified' or 'more important' writers have already pronounced upon the subject. In between are those who find every perspective plausible as they write about it, and lapse into relativism ('it all depends on your point of view') as a conclusion. Against the first of these positions it is important to re-emphasize that the humanities and social sciences are about relational argument, not dogmatic position-taking. For those reluctant to state a position it is worth stressing that your own personal view is important. Many social sciences are relatively young disciplines – there is a relative paucity of good ideas and developed argument, so even undergraduate essays quite often contain valuable insights in their own right. Many of the humanities are subjects where personal reactions to the material you have considered are critical components of intellectual development. No one expects you to be able to *solve* the major controversies you discuss. But it is useful if you can make a reasoned judgement about where the balance of an argument lies.

It is vitally important to make a clear distinction in your writing between those passages where you are presenting someone else's views and those where you are stating your own position. Quite often in argumentative essays students create confusion for their readers by restating conflicting positions as if they were received wisdom or beyond dispute, or views they themselves agreed with. To combat this kind of confusion you should clearly signpost the sequence in which you will discuss viewpoints at the beginning of the essay. Then make sure you signal clearly when you are moving on from discussing one perspective to the next. Finally, be explicit about the point at which you are moving from summarizing other peoples' views into setting out your own approach. It is normally useful to let your own view emerge out of an account of other people's views. If you launch into your introductory paragraph with an assertive position, you may find that you have to repeat the argument later in a more reasoned form.

Matrix Essay Structures

One problem with both analytic and argumentative essays is that it can be difficult to generate enough paragraphs to provide a reasonable framework for an essay. For example, how do you get an eight-paragraph structure if you can only see two different argumentative views on the subject, or three or four analytic aspects of the topic? One solution here is to look at a mixed argumentative and analytic essay, organized on a matrix pattern such as that given below:

Argumentative dimension

	View 1 (e.g. liberal view)	View 2 (e.g. Marxism)
Aspect A (e.g. economic aspect)		
Aspect B (e.g. political aspect)		
Aspect C (e.g. moral/religous aspect)		

Analytic dimension

The sequence in which you describe these paragraphs depends on which dimension you chose to stress most. If you decide that the argumentative dimension is most important then the order of paragraphs will be as in sequence A. Here the complete liberal view is presented, followed by the complete Marxist view.

If, on the other hand, you want to stress the analytic dimension then you could adopt paragraph sequence B. Here liberal and Marxist views of the economic aspect of a problem are presented together; then liberal and Marxist views of the problem's political aspect, and so on. Either way the six core paragraphs plus a short introduction and a conclusion would produce a very tightly structured eight-paragraph essay.

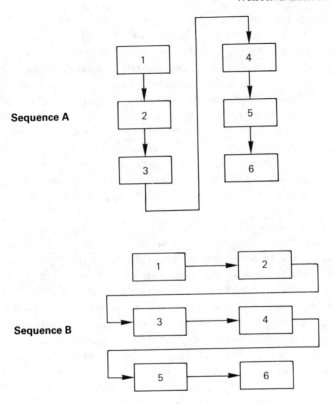

4.4 ESSAY PLANS AND ORGANIZERS

The next step is to produce a detailed plan of how your essay will be organized. Most people jot down a few points in advance of starting to write up their material. But by an 'essay plan' I mean something a good deal more organized and systematic. Two key questions are involved: What function will each paragraph fulfil? And how will you distribute across the paragraphs the ideas and materials generated earlier?

The Paragraph Structure

'The paragraph is a great art form,' said the novelist and

philosopher Iris Murdoch: 'I'm very interested in paragraphs and I write paragraphs very, very carefully.' Paragraphs are key organizing devices which signal to the reader how the author's ideas have been arranged. Starting a new paragraph is a sign that you are changing focus from one aspect of a topic to another. The first sentence of each paragraph is usually read more carefully as a clue to what the whole following chunk of text is about. In fictional material there are good reasons for making paragraphs almost the only organizing device used. The author is trying to persuade readers to 'suspend disbelief', and therefore wishes to avoid reminding you of her role. Even informative chapter headings may be jettisoned in search of a low author profile.

However, there is no very convincing reason why the paragraph is so important as a structuring device in many academic books. Frequent headings and subheadings can fulfil the same role more informatively, hence their use in textbooks and student-orientated materials, where authors are going out of their way to help readers follow their train of thought. Headings work well because they are deliberately obtrusive, rather forcefully reminding the reader of the author's intentions, and it is this quality which also accounts for their omission from other types of material. Academic authors writing primarily for other academics often cultivate a minimal presence merely because it looks conventionally elegant.

Why students rely so much on paragraphing in writing essays is harder to explain. Teachers of English in schools often cultivate a literary style derived from fictional materials, in which headings and subheadings are prohibited in favour of continuous text broken up only by paragraphs. Habits learned at school are then very difficult for people to shed in higher education. Many students are convinced that there is some rule in their subject which forbids using headings in essays. In most cases this view is fallacious. The golden rule is to use as many types of organizer as you need to structure your material clearly. But equally be careful not to overburden your essays with redundant organizers.

The decision about what types of organizers to use, and how many sections of material to distinguish, obviously depends on how long your essay will be. A short paper covering four A4 pages (about 1,200 words) should be structured quite satisfactorily by simply dividing it into around eight paragraphs. However, a longer tutorial essay of eight to ten pages (about 2,500 to 3,000 words) would probably benefit from using some headings to group paragraphs into sections. Obviously the key influence on defining the length of paragraphs is how the material in the essay argument can conveniently be grouped. You need only a manageable number of paragraphs in the essay. Each paragraph should be capable of being absorbed as a coherent unit of thought by the reader. Ideally a paragraph should include several sentences, and cover perhaps half an A4 page (that is, around 100 to 150 words). If a paragraph is longer than about two-thirds of a page, it becomes difficult for readers to grasp the argument in one go. At the same time, with long paragraphs your essay could begin to look understructured.

The two quickest ways to make an essay look completely disorganized are:

(i) *Write without any paragraphs or headings at all.* The essay becomes a seamless web from which the reader must try to separate the main ideas without the help of any signals about the author's intentions. Alternatively,

(ii) *Write each individual sentence as if it were a separate paragraph.* Here any reader will rapidly become be- mused since a four-page essay will have perhaps 50 separate paragraphs, each of which looks as important as the next in signalling what the author judges to be a main idea.

Creating a structure of paragraphs and other organizers entails steering a careful course between these twin poles. The occasional long paragraph may be justified where it cannot conveniently be broken up. But one-sentence paragraphs should always be avoided if at all possible, since they simply devalue the usefulness of paragraphs as an essay organizer.

Sequencing Material

The next step is to take all the materials noted down at the stage of generating ideas and to transfer them on to a reasonably detailed plan of your essay. Take a couple of sheets of paper and divide them up to create between six and ten boxes altogether (depending on how many paragraphs you anticipate in total). For each box, write down an informative heading which reminds you about that paragraph's basic role or purpose. Always avoid purely formal descriptions, such as 'Introduction' or 'Conclusion'. Every paragraph on your plan should be labelled in a way which describes the substantive ideas in that part of the essay.

Now number the paragraphs into a sequence, checking that there is a good reason why paragraph 1 follows paragraph 2 rather than vice versa, and so on through all the paragraphs. It is important not simply to arrange paragraphs in the order in which you first thought of them or already have them set out on your planning sheets. Try always explicitly to reappraise the existing order, asking what alternative arrangements would be feasible. Your earlier decision about what type of essay to write should greatly help to simplify these decisions about the sequencing of ideas. Wherever there remain a number of options, bear in mind that an essay should be cumulative in its impact, it should build an argument, with a clear beginning, middle and end which are easy to distinguish from one another. Maintaining a sense of progress and of development in the argument is essential.

Just as it is important to avoid going round in circles, so you should cover each point as completely as possible, without loose ends that involve you in cross-referencing or in reiterating explanatory material. Be on the look-out for repeated material or for the same basic point restated in different terminology. Always try to group similar or very closely connected points at the same location in the essay. Where three or four small aspects of a viewpoint, or criticisms of an approach, or facets of an example, are explained in the essay, their impact will be considerably reinforced if they are grouped together, and tend to be dissipated if they are made separately. The general rule is to say it once and say it right.

To maintain a sense of development in the argument, and to make each point once as effectively as possible, an essay plan has to build in a 'controlled release' of material. Each

paragraph needs to introduce something distinctive
essay, whether its content consists of arguments,
examples, or other applied analysis. This entails holdin
on information until the stage at which it can be mos   _,
presented and will best add to a coherent argument. For
example, it is particularly important to avoid crudely
summarizing or 'blurting out' key substantive arguments in
your introduction, since this will create a sense of repetition
when the same points are fully stated later on.

An introductory paragraph should be used only for three
purposes.

(a) **To give essential definitions of key concepts** included in
the essay question. Let me emphasize again that you should be
very restrictive in incorporating definitional material from the
question analysis stage into the essay itself. Work out the
meaning of concepts for your own purposes, so that you can
avoid making mistakes and can write in an informed way. But
only a few bits of the work you do to clarify your own thinking
will need to be explicitly defined in the essay itself.

(b) **To respecify the essay question somewhat**, if this is
necessary. Where a question is so broad as to be potentially
unanswerable, then you should explain explicitly how you have
interpreted the question so as to make it more manageable.
Similarly if a question could be open-ended (pp. 85–6, you
should indicate what you see as the core problem to be tackled.

(c) **To signpost the sequence of material in the rest of the
essay.** You should aim to orientate the reader to the framework
of topics which you will be tackling. But do not summarize the
substantive arguments given later. At degree level it is usually
worth avoiding the heavy-handed philosophy of: 'Tell them
what you're going to tell them, then tell them, then tell them
what you've told them.'

Essays written without advanced planning often feature very
lengthy introductions, where the author engages in a kind of
'phoney war' of promising to tackle the question in just a
minute or so. One way to avoid such protracted ground-
clearing paragraphs is to set yourself a restrictive guideline,
such as a personal rule of thumb that none of your introductory

paragraphs will be longer than half a page (about ten lines). Necessary material which cannot fit within such a limit (for example, lengthy definitions which really do have to be included) must then be treated not as part of the introduction but as part of the substantive argument. Some teachers even suggest avoiding introductions altogether, in favour of launching immediately into your core argument. This approach has the advantage of forcing you to work your definitions of concepts into the fabric of your main arguments. However, some signposts are always useful in any reasonably complex argument, and many essay questions do need some specification before you launch off in full flood. A short and punchy introduction can be very useful in setting an essay off on the right footing.

One final caveat on sequencing material may be useful. Controlled release of information does not mean that you should hold back unnecessarily on stating your central arguments, or that you should save up all your most original or substantive points until the end of the essay. Because most of your personal arguments will grow out of criticisms of the existing literature, there is a certain natural tendency for them to enter at a later stage. But you should beware of constructing essay plans which follow a 'dance of the seven veils' pattern, in which layers of irrelevance are progressively torn aside to reveal the core argument only in the conclusion. Getting into this habit of writing can be a liability in unseen written exams, where time constraints require you to move speedily into the core of an answer (pp. 157–60). It is possible to maintain momentum while yet moving into your major arguments early on in the essay.

4.5 COMPOSITION AND STYLE

Once you begin composing actual text new concerns come into focus, particularly difficulties of composition and of finding an appropriate writing style.

Writing-up Text

There is a very wide gap between planning an essay and writing out the argument in full. However effectively you generate ideas and analyse the question, whatever type of essay you choose to write, and however extensively you detail the organizing structure of the argument and the contents of each paragraph – converting these ideas into finished prose remains a major problem. Some common and intractable difficulties are motivational. Essay plans which seem competent and innovative on your advance sheets turn out to look routine or ordinary when written up in full. Difficult passages which seemed manageable on the outline become impassable roadblocks to further progress when you cannot express the essential points of an argument. If you get the impression that the essay is not going well, it may be difficult to nerve yourself to go on producing the appropriate quota of joined-up handwriting.

'I always write when I'm inspired,' remarked the author Peter de Vries: 'And I see to it that I'm inspired at nine o'clock every morning.' This philosophy perfectly expresses the point of extensive essay planning. However discouraging the task of converting a plan into text may seem, it is far less of a problem than sitting down with a blank sheet of paper to construct an essay argument in your head as you go along. Planning can never get rid of the uphill slog of writing up. But it does help greatly to reduce the 'threshold' you have to surmount in getting started, and to smooth over the 'hiccups' which will inevitably occur at one or more later stages in the composition.

A number of apparently trivial steps can greatly facilitate writing up.

(a) **Compose text in ways which you can change easily.** Many students still write down essays in a 'neat', compressed format learned at school, for example, using single-spacing on both sides of the paper. This practice means that if you make a mistake or a wrong turning you may have to rewrite up to 500 words in order to put things right. Instead write or type drafts in double spacing (so you can insert small amounts of new material later using the alternate blank lines), and on one side of the paper only (which reduces your words per page to perhaps 200, and hence makes it easier to revise paragraphs without rewriting preceding or succeeding material as well).

(b) **Do not be too obsessive about the finished appearance of your work.** Unlike schoolteachers, who can have fixed ideas about a 'neat' format in which written work should be produced, most lecturers in higher education will not mind reading essays in any format, so long as it is legible and makes clear the boundaries of paragraphs. They will always appreciate not having text presented in a dense mass of cramped handwriting, which is hard to read and hard to add comments to. So it is vital that you shed some of the worst inhibitions about handing in 'untidy work' which many schools spend years inculcating into their pupils, but which function chiefly to inhibit your readiness to revise anything once it is written out.

Of course, this is not to say that you should ignore opportunities to improve the presentation of your work if at all possible. Clear handwriting, or better still typed essays, neatly corrected mistakes, proper margins for comments – all of these help make a good impression on tutors. Accurate spelling is also important. Even the best planned argument can be made to look quite silly if key terms are constantly misspelled. But presentation should always take second place to securing the best substantive argument. You should never be put off rearranging paragraphs in a completed essay by a fear that lecturers will object to slight defects in presentation. Perhaps the best way to compose text is by using a word-processor, which allows you to rearrange and rephrase material at the touch of a button, and to print a 'clean' version (p. 127). Without such sophisticated tools, you can still make do by using correcting fluid and physically 'cutting and pasting' passages back together in a new sequence. The key thing is not to lock yourself into one sequence of presenting material, or to waste time trying to disguise or justify finished passages of text where the argument is defective.

(c) **Keep your essay plan under review as you write.** Converting any plan into text invariably raises some problems or avenues of development which you had not foreseen, so you should be prepared to change tack, or to discuss topics in a slightly different order. For example, you will often find that material to which you allocated only one paragraph at the planning stage takes a good deal longer to set out, necessitating adding new paragraphs. Frequently the demands of writing finished prose stimulate further thought and digging among your sources, which in turn may trigger new insights. Similarly, some paragraphs which looked viable on the plan can end up looking weak in their full text form, and hence might be better assimilated into surrounding paragraphs.

Style

In much degree-level work achieving an effective writing style is a precondition for receiving high marks for essays or in exams. Only in the technical social sciences where mathematical or analytic ability is critical will a poor style cease to be a handicap. The converse of these propositions, of course, does not hold. Good style alone cannot suffice. It is a necessary but not a sufficient condition of achieving a good degree.

What counts as 'good style'? There is a considerable range of opinion about this, both across disciplines and across individual teachers and students. Ultimately 'style' decisions are personal ones. But three generalizations can be made.

(a) **Picture your audience** and write in a manner appropriate to them. Just as pitching your essay at too basic a level involves you in redescribing material which could be taken as read, so there is no sense in which adding inappropriate phrasing at particular points will strengthen an argument. At degree level you need to avoid devaluing your presentation by including purple passages, exaggerated sentiments, or 'over the top' statements. This is not to prescribe deliberate blandness. But you should test each phrase or sentence as you write it – asking whether it advances the argument, whether you want to commit yourself fully to the viewpoint it expresses, whether it is accurate, whether it is fair, and what sort of reaction it is likely to produce. An 'extreme' statement of a view is perfectly acceptable, so long as it passes these tests. Be sure that you are saying precisely what you want to say, and expressing views which you would be happy to support if queried.

(b) Other things being equal, **'good style' is concise, clear, and simple.** Good writers employ an extensive vocabulary, including technical terms where it is useful to do so. Necessary 'jargon' should not be avoided simply in search of a more traditionally literary appearance, since a technical vocabulary is usually much more precise than ordinary language equivalents. 'Good style' usually entails phrasing viewpoints in the most direct and accessible language, for example, by writing in short sentences. Short sentences can be more easily controlled and manipulated than those held together by complex grammatical devices. If qualifying clauses are necessary, they can be best accommodated by placing them either at the beginning or the end of sentences, where they will least disrupt the flow of language. Arguments are best presented using active rather than passive language, and verbs rather than nouns.

The key thing is to tailor your approach to the task in hand, and to avoid pretentiousness, 'contrived' phrasing, deliberate flamboyance or pomposity, and overwriting in general. There are occasions when a very studied style may be legitimate, particularly in those humanities disciplines where using the evocative or emotive power of language is most important. But in most cases the best way of expressing a point is to write it conversationally, as you might say it if the person for whom you are writing was in the room with you. If you would feel a bit unnatural saying what you have just written, then perhaps it is over-rhetorical?

Part of the push to overembellish writing is an anxiety to differentiate one's style, to add something more to the arguments derived from your sources, and to write up the essay in a way which is original. This anxiety is well grounded to the extent that many people find it difficult to re-express some of the materials they have read in a different manner from the initial author. Getting out from under the shadow of major thinkers and previous critics certainly requires that you set out the arguments involved in your own terms. But you can be confident that if you fully 'translate' other people's thinking, you will also achieve an individual style of your own, without extra efforts being necessary.

As for a more thorough-going 'originality', stressing personal reactions to fundamental problems, this quality is a product of your whole way of approaching your course of study. There is no sense in which genuinely original insights can be added as a purely stylistic gloss to otherwise undistinguished materials. These knowledge or argumentative advances are conditioned far more by your success in gathering information, critically analysing concepts, and following through the early stages of essay planning than by the way in which you write up the finished essay.

Summary of Suggestions: Writing Essays

1. Write essays regularly, and do not delay completing an essay in a new subject for too long (p. 80).

2. Write in your own way, to maximize relevance to your essay question and to get more accurate feedback on how to improve your performance. Be persistent in seeking feedback from teachers on your writing (p. 80).

3. Always write essays in response to questions, rather than around a vague title (p. 82).

4. Write several short essays fairly quickly, rather than long ones, in order to cover more topics in a form less remote from exam answers (p. 82).

5. Beware of hypnotically repeating a question's phrasing without analysing the concepts involved (p. 83).

6. Apply techniques for analysing concepts to clarify all the ideas in the essay question. Do not focus just on the overtly technical concepts: pay attention also to the everyday linking words which make the question distinctive (p. 84).

7. 'Brainstorm' round the essay question for a short period,

generating ideas without criticizing them. Eliminate ideas which are clearly irrelevant to the question later on, when you have generated a whole field of possible ideas (p. 84).

8. Try writing out the opposite of the question, or getting clear what it is *not* asking (p. 85).

9. Make sure that you recognize open-ended questions which need to be limited in scope if relevance is to be maintained (p. 85).

10. Try to avoid writing simply 'descriptive' essays – including chronologies, guidebook essays, or those which summarize the views of a random sequence of authors (p. 88).

11. To write more analytic essays, use your own mental categories to subdivide material, and to select what is relevant for your argument. Use periodization to tackle chronological topics. Or divide a complex subject into systematic subsections, or separate causal processes – any of these devices can allow you to write analytic essays (p. 89).

12. To write well-organized argumentative essays, ask what opposing or different views there could be of the subject. What kind of controversy could there be about it? (p. 92).

13. In writing argumentative essays, take care to use accurate descriptions of the different viewpoints. Also make it quite clear when you are summarizing someone else's argument, and when you are stating your own views (p. 94).

14. Combinations of argumentative and analytic dimensions can be used to generate a matrix structure for essays. Examine different ways of ordering paragraphs before you fix on an essay structure (p. 96).

15. Use as many organizing devices as you need to structure an essay, but do not overburden it with unnecessary organizers. Paragraphs are the major essay organizers, but use headings in longer essays, or wherever they help to clarify the argument (p. 98).

16. Write paragraphs as coherent units of thought. Avoid very short one- or two-sentence paragraphs, but equally keep paragraphs of manageable size (p. 99).

17. Sequence materials in your essay so as to make each major set of points at one particular stage, to avoid repetition, and to develop the argument cumulatively (p. 100).

18. Use introductions only to give essential definitions, to respecify the essay question, and to give some signposts about the sequence of topics covered in the rest of the essay (p. 101).

19. Keep introductions deliberately short. Keep definitions to the minimum needed. Get into the core arguments of your essay as early as possible (p. 102).

20. Aim for a 'controlled release' of information throughout the essay. Avoid blurting out the substantive argument too early in a crude way. But equally, do not make your core arguments appear only in the conclusions (p. 100).

21. Write up your essay text in a form which you can change easily. And do not worry so much about neatness that you are unwilling to cut up and resequence paragraphs when you have finished. Keep your essay plan under review as you write (p. 103).

22. To achieve a good style in essay writing, picture your audience as you write, and choose the simplest, clearest and most concise way of expressing your arguments (p. 105).

5 Writing Dissertations

Reading Guide

If your degree includes a dissertation option or requirement, read this chapter well before you have to start work on your project. Topics covered are:

1. The most common types of dissertation requirement.
2. Literature reviews.
3. Case-studies or applied analyses.
4. The mechanics of planning and completing dissertations.

An appendix explains different types of referencing system.

5.1 DISSERTATION REQUIREMENTS

During the last ten years more and more courses in the humanities and social sciences have expected students to produce at least one dissertation as part of their degree. This general movement undoubtedly reflects an increasing awareness of the limited range of skills and knowledge which can be accurately gauged by any one assessment system, such as the traditional unseen written exams. A dissertation provides an opportunity for students to demonstrate some originality in identifying a topic or a line of argument, and to follow up their insight with a more systematic piece of research work. In addition there has been a steady expansion in the number of students who take a one-year Diploma or Master's course (less frequently of two years) in addition to their first degree. All of these post-graduate courses include at least one dissertation, and many include quite lengthy term-papers in their assessment systems. There are two main levels of dissertation in undergraduate or masters degrees.

(a) **Long essays or mini-dissertations** require students to choose one of a small number of pre-set questions and frame a response in greater depth than ordinary tutorial or class essays. Normally there is a fairly restrictive word limit of around 2,000 to 5,000 words (which is about 8 to 15 sides of double-spaced typescript on A4 paper). This sort of mini-dissertation is distinctive because there is no onus on the student to define a topic, merely to frame an interesting answer to a question already set by teachers. Because there is a pre-set focus and a finite effort limit, writing long essays is quite similar to ordinary written assignments. But other features raise similar problems to longer dissertations, such as the need to undertake more systematic research, generate your own literature sources, organize a more complex argument, and avoid committing disproportionate effort to the dissertation.

(b) **Dissertations proper** require students to define their own topic, get it approved by their tutor, and then write around 10,000 to 15,000 words on the subject. This exercise is a much more open-ended activity. Because students are searching simultaneously for an interesting or original question, and for an effective response, it is particularly easy to take on too ambitious a programme of study or research. In practice, 10,000 words is just 30 pages of double-spaced typing on A4 paper, closer to the average article in an academic journal than to the much bigger theses produced for research degrees.

Research theses, which are not discussed here, generally have an upper word limit in the range between 50,000 words (for an M.Phil.) to 100,000 words (for a Ph.D.). This range is between 150 and 300 typescript A4 pages. Although M.Phils do not, and doctorates need not, make an original contribution to knowledge, there is still a heavy premium on undertaking empirical work in an uncharted area, or on generating some kind of theoretical advance. Research theses also have to be defended in an oral examination. Both aspects of research work tend to generate a search for an extremely narrow topic which the student can make exclusively her own.

Students can undertake many different types of project in order to fulfil dissertation requirements. The traditional emphasis on individual written work has been dented (especially in the polytechnics) by the growth of group project work, which is now quite common at the first-degree level. In fields such as music, painting, sculpture, drama, film, journalism and communication studies, 'live' or demonstration projects are now commonplace at first- and master's-degree level. Given this diversity of method and purpose, it is not possible to cover substantive projects in this chapter, except in so far as one result of project work involves writing an individual report. For useful advice on completing projects see Ashman and George (1982), Chapters 7 and 8.

For the rest, dissertation projects always involve some research which goes beyond the normal (fairly perfunctory) process of reading and preparing for a tutorial or class essay in some respect. There are two common ways of doing this. The first is to complete a literature review, and the second is to undertake a case-study of some kind.

5.2 LITERATURE REVIEWS

Literature reviews are based on a systemic reading of existing academic writing on a particular topic. While a routine essay often relies on no more than half a dozen secondary sources, literature reviews are based on many times this number. The aim is to survey and report on a reasonably large or complex field of work, in the process developing some themes to make the review distinctive. Most students encounter plenty of possible topics during their course on which they would not mind conducting some more intensive research. Familiarity with professional academics' review articles means that defining a style is straightforward. Two big problems remain – how to conduct a reasonably comprehensive search for relevant documentation, and how to give your review a distinctive theme or angle of its own.

Documentation Searches

Almost by definition, a literature review cannot be better than the materials surveyed – 'garbage in' implies 'garbage out'. Of course, the converse does not apply – it is quite easy for a literature review to be worse than the field surveyed. Indeed the more developed the literature being covered, the more difficult it may be to understand parts of the argument in the original sources, (especially where arguments have technical or algebraic sections). These considerations indicate some general dilemmas in choosing a subject area for a literature review. If you choose a very small or unstudied topic it will be easier to be comprehensive in your coverage, but unearthing possible sources may be more difficult. Reviewing an already extensive academic literature expands the range of materials you have to cover, but makes it easier to find at least a 'critical mass' of writing. Similarly if you choose a low-level or undeveloped area in which to review progress, it is easier to understand the materials, but more difficult to find anything interesting to say. Opting for a review of a better populated field increases the effort involved in simply précising what you have read, and may create other kinds of difficulties in defining an innovative angle on the debate.

Generating information for a literature review dissertation essentially requires a more extensive and systematic application of the suggestions made in section 2.1. Procedures which you may rarely have time to use with ordinary essays are more practicable. In particular, a search through recent volumes of leading journals often throws up new articles and reviews of relevant books which you might not otherwise find. Similarly, an on-line computer search using carefully specified appropriate keywords can get a documentation search off to a flying start, providing that your library offers this service and that you can afford the charges usually levied.

Reviewing from an Angle

When working on a dissertation it is quite easy to become overorientated to the formal requirements involved – so that you worry overmuch about quite technical issues, such as the degree regulations, or the referencing system you should use. However, the crucial determinant of whether a dissertation is successful is almost always whether the project has a clear rationale, and is written in a way which is interesting for readers. In literature reviews the critical element most frequently missing is an explicit angle or theme – a sense of what the author wants to do differently or what insights she hopes to gain from completing the review. Since it is very hard to think up and write down new and original theory in most areas of the humanities or social sciences, it is quite sensible to start by first considering what other authors have written on a subject, and then deriving some more personal criticisms or arguments. However, there is little point in starting a review and hoping that an angle will emerge as you go along. The bulk of the dissertation may then consist of an undistinctive summary of what you have read, and your expected original elements may simply not materialize.

Therefore it is important that you specify at the outset the angle from which you propose to survey a literature. This step needs to be taken long before you actually start writing up a draft. Once identified, your individual approach should inform the selection of materials included throughout the dissertation. It should not be a 'surprise' element which arrives unsignposted in the concluding paragraphs. Where you define both the question to be asked and the answer provided, do not create a mismatch between the key questions posed at the start of your work, the discussion of other authors in the middle, and the more original insights at the end. If you know what your own personal contribution will be, then arrange the early parts of the dissertation to lead up naturally to your central criticisms or ideas. Similarly, there is no point in reviewing a mass of authors if this renders your coverage superficial and means that your personal contribution relates to only a tiny fraction of the material covered.

When deciding an area for a literature review check to see if the field in question has already been surveyed. Review articles in journals are the most useful starting place, for unlike the textbooks they give you an idea of the kind of style which could be appropriate for your dissertation. In addition, they are normally much more up-to-date than textbook discussions. Secondly, you need to ask what you could do differently from existing literature reviews. This question cannot easily be solved by finding a field which is entirely unpopulated by reviews. It is often more difficult to start from a blank canvas than to react to a previous pattern of commentary. Perhaps the ideal situation is one where a field of study has been reviewed in the past, but where an accumulation of newer work has not so far been surveyed. Similarly some areas of academic work may be well developed (and hence surveyed) in one country but less well known or synthesized in another. For example, a review of British literature in terms of American perspectives can often be useful. In the humanities there are often insights to be made by contrasting, say, Anglo-American literatures with West European approaches. Comparing empirical debates across countries or time periods may be easier than handling divergent theoretical perspectives, which tend to focus on radically different phenomena. But the analytic gains obtainable from cross-theory comparisons can also be considerable. The general rule is always to look for elements present in the existing literature which could usefully be brought into an unusual conjunction or synthesized in a new survey.

5.3 CASE-STUDY DISSERTATIONS

Case-studies cover a bewildering variety of activities. Library-based case-studies all involve undertaking some applied analysis – for example, local historical, social or political research; reanalysing primary texts in literature or philosophy; or consulting original sources, such as manuscripts (or replica manuscripts) in history. Many case-studies involve undertaking fieldwork such as physical geography field trips, archaeology 'digs', student surveys in sociology or anthropology, interviewing local decision-makers in politics or public administration, or social work placements in social policy and administration. Normally the material generated by case-studies of many kinds is original in the sense that the precise information obtained was not previously recorded. Of course, it may not be novel or interesting information. Indeed, the results obtained are often quite predictable from the existing knowledge base. Nonetheless the essence of case-study work is that students break out of the circle of secondary material within which most higher education operates, and instead make direct contact with primary source materials –

which in the case of fieldwork they have generated themselves from scratch.

The stimulus behind case-study theses is usually empirical curiosity. For example, students who have encountered particular explanations in their coursework want to see how far these can be applied to the experience of their own area or country. In history or literary fields, case-studies often involve the reanalysis of texts, records or other primary sources looking for new kinds of evidence or new meanings passed over by earlier studies, or extending a pattern of analysis developed elsewhere to some new text or source.

Models for Case-Study Projects

Case-study proposals often assume that if the author proposes to analyse a hitherto undocumented phenomenon, then adding to the sum of knowledge is justification enough for going ahead. But 'knowledge' is not a rubbish heap of unconnected 'facts'. It is a set of linked-up insights. So before proceeding with a case study, it is vitally important to ask what it is a case of, and how it can be usefully linked up with or related to existing knowledge.

Perhaps the best way to appreciate how a case-study can be usefully undertaken is to look at examples already carried out by academic authors. Of course, you need to make allowances for the much more sophisticated investigations undertaken by professional academics, especially if empirical work in your field is conducted mainly by large grant-funded research projects. Working on your own, in a period spanning at best a few months, and without access to funding or elaborate research tools, you are not going to be able to carry out anything much resembling the paradigm studies in your field. This gap is reduced if work in your field predominantly reflects the individual efforts of academics snatching a rare term or two's sabbatical to undertake some systematic information gathering. But even here, published authors usually have far more experience in conducting empirical enquiries.

To see how best to bridge this gap, a useful next step is to look at earlier successful dissertations by students on your course, which should be properly stored and filed in your department.

Your tutor should be able to indicate a number of good efforts from earlier years which show what is feasible. The larger your course or department the greater the likelihood that someone has already done something like the case-study which you are proposing. If your course is rather small, especially at Masters level, you may be left more to your own resources, with few previous dissertations in your area and not much staff experience about the prospects and pitfalls of student-conducted research. It is difficult to overstate the value of skimming one or two successful dissertations close to your topic in developing a case-study of your own. A potential for reinventing the wheel exists in all subjects. However original your approach, however unusual your problems, or however restrictive your time or research resources, you will usually find that someone has tackled an analagous situation and come up with some useful ideas or solutions.

Linking Applied Research with Broader Themes

There are two basic ways of linking up your own empirical research or applied analysis with the broader theoretical themes and empirical concerns of the existing literature. The most commonly used model is **a focus-down approach** (Figure 5.1). Here the dissertation starts with a chapter or so

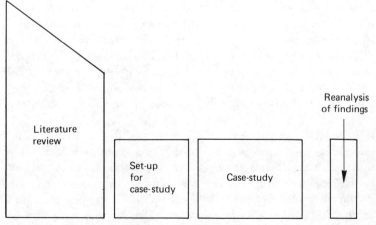

Figure 5.1: The 'focus-down' model for case-study dissertations

which discusses some wide-ranging empirical themes or theoretical controversies. Students often feel that they are duty bound to begin by demonstrating wide reading and a knowledge of theoretical disputes in their field. Consequently these mini-literature reviews can become very long-winded affairs, covering a canvas much broader than the issues which will be directly addressed in later sections. There is then an abrupt change of scale or tone in which the macro-themes of the opening chapter are succeeded by the micro-concerns of the case-study itself. The empirical analysis usually has to be introduced before anything of substantive interest can be said, so that the dissertation in a sense restarts at this point along a different track from that followed so far. The theoretical discussion and the presentation of empirical results are thus separated by the set-up material for the case-study. Finally when the substantive results of the case-study have been presented, the author may or may not return to the broader themes of the first chapter in order to consider how her results connect up with them. Sometimes this reanalysis is omitted, as if the significance of the case-study findings and their relationship with the opening themes are both too obvious to need detailed discussion.

Despite being very widely used, the 'focus-down' approach adds considerably to the authoring difficulties inherent in completing any longer piece of work. It tends to produce dissertations where only a small proportion of the theories introduced in the opening chapter are ever directly addressed by the case-study itself – giving the impression that the discussion of broader themes has been 'tacked on' to dignify an otherwise mundane piece of work. Setting out the theoretical scenery on a broad canvas also consumes so much space that students quite often barely analyse their most interesting results. If the initial literature review is instead kept within a tight limit, it can appear crude, since at this stage there is no clear basis for restricting the scope of discussion to manageable limits. Above all the 'focus-down' approach usually does not build to any impressive conclusion. Big concerns are introduced only to progressively drop out of the picture again as the scope of discussion narrows. It is all too easy for the dissertation to end 'not with a bang but a whimper'.

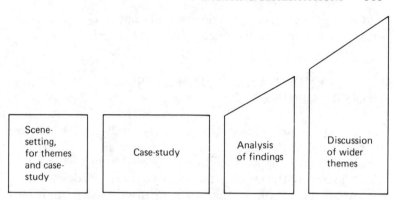

Figure 5.2: The 'opening-out' model for case-study dissertations

An alternative model avoiding many of these pitfalls is **the opening-out approach** (Figure 5.2). Here the dissertation starts with a short scene-setting chapter. Without going through any extended review of literature, it nonetheless sets out in a concise and straightforward way the problems which will be tackled. You can often take it for granted that readers are familiar with the basic literature on the subject, but you should always bring out your rationale for conducting the case-study. Even if your dissertation is likely to be read only by one or two examiners, it is important to make it interesting and to provide readers with incentives to persevere. A set-up chapter can also get across some information about the selection of the case-study materials or locale, which is usually necessary. Next the substantive empirical or applied analysis of the case-study itself is presented, making clear the central findings but without discussing their significance at this stage. The third section analyses the significance of these results, set against the briefly specified problematic of the opening chapter. A procedure of this kind provides the springboard for you to broaden out your analysis and to discuss the wider issues raised by your findings. Unlike the 'focus down' approach, this pattern ensures that you concentrate discussion of broader themes only on those areas touched on by your own empirical results. In addition you only discuss general theoretical ideas once in the concluding chapter. The outcome should be a greater sense of the integral connection between the theoretical and applied aspects of the dissertation, and a more coherent orchestration of its different elements.

5.4 PLANNING AND COMPLETING DISSERTATIONS

Gathering information (Chapter 2), analysing concepts (Chapter 3), or devising an essay plan (Chapter 4) – are all involved in preparing a dissertation. Five additional stages are also entailed in carrying out a longer piece of writing: developing a synopsis; timetabling the work involved; using multiple organizers; referencing; and producing a typescript.

Developing a Synopsis

In clarifying your initial ideas for a topic, you will need to write a synopsis – a brief preliminary account of your dissertation. A synopsis should set out clearly the key problems to be addressed, the way you propose to explore them, the kinds of information to be generated or the main source materials to be used, and the primary methods of research to be employed. Ideally it should also sketch a tentative sequence of chapters, perhaps with a paragraph or so of text to fill out each chapter title. If this is too difficult to accomplish in an initial synopsis (as it invariably is with research theses), then you will need to compose further synopses which do outline the role of each chapter. Once you have these basic descriptions, each chapter needs to be further subdivided into a number of sections or subheadings, depending on how long the chapters will be.

Many students find the idea of writing synopses an intimidating one. Their idea is apparently to (somehow) 'do the research' first, and find out later how to organize it in text form. Sometimes this reluctance to plan is inherited from an experience of 'muddling through' on ordinary undergraduate essays with no very clear forethought. But in dealing with much longer pieces of work it is invariably a recipe for disaster. At other times, people hold back from handing in a synopsis which has to be accepted by their tutor before they can proceed to do extended work on their dissertation, viewing the topic proposal itself as part of their assessment. Here, producing a synopsis entails 'going public' on your ideas, and (normally) encountering at least some critical feedback. All of these reactions are perfectly understandable but unwise.

Synopses are invaluable in helping you sort out your ideas in several ways. First, it is always useful to set out project proposals formally. We can all go on mentally balancing far more ideas and possibilities in our heads than we can actually set out in a coherent fashion on paper. If you confine yourself to oral discussions with tutors or fellow students, you are unlikely to straighten out your ideas. Second, your tutors cannot respond at all effectively to an oral presentation of your ideas. Consequently without a full synopsis your dissertation may be very advanced before you get any serious commentary on it. Critical feedback on your dissertation at a late stage is intensely discouraging since you have expended most of your efforts already, and there is little you can do in the remaining time to change your draft. But at an early stage tutors' criticisms are much more helpful and much easier to accommodate. They often indicate short-cuts to take or dead-ends to avoid.

One way to overcome hang-ups in writing a synopsis is to think of it as a rolling process in which you produce a succession of three- or four-page 'disposable' summaries which you then rethink further. For example, if a chapter merits just a few lines of text in your current draft, try jotting down in random fashion all the ideas you have about the topic until you have filled a sheet or two of paper. Then number these ideas into a rough sequence, which can be rewritten as a proper plan when the major ideas involved have emerged more clearly. Developing the synopsis stage by stage from your first cryptic and disorganized thoughts to a properly organized final plan can be quite painless so long as you do not invest too much self-esteem in the early versions. Today's synopsis (like today's newspaper) is often tomorrow's fishpaper.

Timetabling the Work

You may have to define your synopsis several months before the submission deadline for the completed dissertation. But at least some of the intervening period may be effectively blanked out for doing research because you are simultaneously completing coursework or revising for exams. In many undergraduate degrees and some master's courses, dissertations have to be submitted in the early summer (around June), virtually simultaneously with a cluster of end-of-year examinations. If the dissertation gets delayed, it eats into the revision and examination period for the written papers. Good timetabling here means finishing the dissertation well before the onset of the examination season, for example during the Easter vacation.

In other master's courses the dissertation has to be submitted in late summer (around September), two to three months after the end-of-year exams. Many students appreciate these eight weeks or so to concentrate solely on their dissertations. But in practice this period rapidly gets eaten away – by post-exam celebrations, holiday plans and generally sunny weather. In addition many tutors disappear and often libraries close for substantial stretches of the long vacation. If your research involves interviewing people in outside organizations, July and August can also be frustrating months. So your 'eight clear weeks' can thus easily reduce to less than half this amount. Good timetabling here entails overcoming the temptation to postpone doing anything on the dissertation until the exams have been completed. The summer period is only really useful for writing-up and producing a typescript. Time-consuming case-study research, or finding literature sources, must be completed before the exam season. And the summer is the worst time to work out or reappraise the basic themes of your dissertation, because there is less chance of getting feedback from teaching staff in the holiday season.

Whatever type of dissertation you are working on, some timetabling rules of thumb are worth bearing in mind.

(a) **Set a restrictive limit to your introductory period of reading and theoretical clarification.** Do not delay doing some substantive research for too long. Especially if your work involves empirical investigation or applied analysis, you should spend no more than a fifth of your total period for dissertation work on producing synopses and preliminary work. Clarifying your own ideas sufficiently to be able to begin empirical

WRITING DISSERTATIONS   123

enquiry is important. But premature definition of an overelaborate theoretical position is a real danger unless you have done some applied work to support it. Academic authors frequently write up books or papers as if they had first developed a complete theoretical approach, and then on conducting empirical research discover (surprise, surprise!) that their model was vindicated. In practice, it is far more likely that the authors began work with some ideas, which on investigation had to be considerably modified. In applied research, defining a theoretical position is normally an iterative process. Initial ideas suggest a research avenue. Empirical work then partially invalidates or does not fit with these ideas. The initial model is revised and reapplied, and so on. At the end of several rounds of this process a reasonable fit between theory and applied research is achieved. Too long a period of abstract theorizing or literature reviewing could mean that when you do eventually carry out some fieldwork or consult primary materials, many of the ideas which you have laboriously accumulated prove irrelevant, unoperationalizable, or plain wrong.

(b) **Write up your findings as you go along.** Your timetable should not schedule long periods for applied research and nothing else. You should make allowances for writing quick first drafts of each section of the research as you complete them. This procedure lets you check whether the results are turning out as originally envisaged. The shorter your dissertation the less important this advice. But even in a short dissertation, you should avoid long gaps between carrying out applied work and writing up your findings. For example, on a master's course it would be a bad idea to conduct a series of interviews in the Easter vacation, but not to write them up until after the summer examinations. By this stage you will have forgotten some of your impressions of the people involved or the context of the interviews. The longer your dissertation, the more writing up as you go along is essential, since the potential loss of information from the research period is much greater. In addition, it is important to produce first drafts in a chapter format and to an appropriate length in order to monitor whether you are staying within word limits, and whether you are gathering too much or too little information. Some major difficulties in completing dissertations are caused by 'overkills', where people produce far more material than the permitted word length. Equally bear in mind the possibility that your topic or approach may not be sustainable at the right level. Writing up as you go along will demonstrate early on if you need to cut your losses and change topics rather than plodding on to a poor mark or a referral.

(c) **At least a quarter of your available dissertation time needs to be set aside for producing a final draft.** In an average master's course where you can devote three or four months to producing your dissertation, at least a month will be needed solely for converting your notes and first draft empirical sections into final form.

(d) **Make time allowances from the outset for having your dissertation typed, proof-read and bound** where necessary. The mechanical operations of getting a clean, checked and copied typescript usually take at least two weeks.

Using Multiple Organizers

In dissertations, unlike essays, paragraphing is never enough. To present ideas in a clearly structured way a more developed set of organizers is necessary, even in a mini-dissertation of 5,000 words. The range of additional organizers available includes chapter divisions, numbered subsections, numbered figures and diagrams, one or more levels of unnumbered subheadings, a contents page, and a brief advance description of the structure of later sections. Of course, additional organizers can be overdone. Just as the value of paragraphing in normal essays can be effectively undermined by writing one-sentence paragraphs, so headings and other organizers must be used sparingly if they are to retain their usefulness. But properly deployed they should allow readers to scan quickly through a dissertation and discern its basic organizational structure. And they should help you to present material in a controlled way, with a minimum of extra verbal signposting in the text itself.

To some extent, decisions about how many organizers are needed are matters of personal taste. But a useful rule of thumb to bear in mind is that some kind of heading will be needed every 1,000 to 2,000 words (i.e. every 3 to 6 pages of A4 double-spaced typescript). Within these sections it should be relatively easy to structure the argument using paragraphing alone, and for readers to follow the pattern of organization. But beyond about 2,000 words some sectional indicators are needed. If you have several different types of headings they should be ordered into a hierarchy which will cue readers to their relative importance. There are many ways in which this can be accomplished using capital letters and/or underlining, or numbered subsections (2.1, 2.2, etc.) inside chapters. The longer your dissertation, the more care is needed to establish a clear set of organizers.

(a) **For a mini-dissertation of around 5,000 words,** it should be enough to split the essay into around four sections, and to give an indication of their sequence in a few lines during the opening paragraphs. There should be no appendices.

(b) **In a dissertation of 10–15,000 words** you will need between 3 and 5 chapters, with a short (one- or two-page) summary of their organizing rationale included in the introduction. Those substantive chapters which are longer than about 2,000 words will probably benefit from at least one order of subheadings. There should be no need for more than two orders of headings overall (i.e. section 2.1, but not section 2.1.1). A contents page at the beginning should always list the chapter headings, and one order of subheadings if used. Tables and figures should be labelled in the same way (i.e. all as 'Table . .' or as 'Figure . .'), and numbered in a single sequence throughout the text, unless they are extremely numerous. One appendix may be useful, for example, to set out large volumes of data, to describe the sources or research methods used, or to list interviewees.

Referencing

In writing dissertations a great deal more care needs to be taken over citing literature than is the case with ordinary essays. However relaxed your tutors may normally be about referencing, dissertations are expected to give proper details of sources used, quotations, and so on. Inadequate referencing will always lose marks: by contrast scrupulous referencing, documenting wide reading, always strengthens examiners' confidence in giving higher marks. The detail to be included in footnotes needs to be decided early in your researches. Carefully record the page location of any quotations or other reference points when making notes on sources. For modern works a page number is sufficient. But for older literary or philosophical sources, which are published in many different editions, you usually need to cite the chapter, subsection or paragraph number as well, so that examiners could turn up the reference even if they have a different edition of the work from the one you are using. If you include a quotation in your notes or in your text without simultaneously taking down its precise location, you may spend a lot of time trying to find the missing data. So check early on what requirements you have to observe, preferably against a detailed style sheet. Alternatively, consult a previous year's dissertation to see how the author has handled the referencing.

There are two basic ways of handling referencing information, traditional footnotes, and Harvard referencing, which are described in the Appendix to this chapter. If these approaches are not familiar, you should study the following guidelines quite carefully. Basically **footnotes** work by inserting small superscript numbers into your text, which guide the reader to a note given at the end of the page, chapter or dissertation. The note contains all the details of sources. Since footnotes are numbered in sequence, considerable work is required to change their sequence around. By contrast **the Harvard system** works by inserting the author names and dates of sources directly in the main text, enclosed in brackets. The reader then looks up the reference directly in a comprehensive list of the sources cited, the bibliography. Harvard references are easier to change, but they tend to be more visible and interrupt the main text more, especially if a lot of literature is cited at any one point.

Whichever referencing system you decide to use, follow that style in making your own notes from the outset. To compile **a bibliography**, you need a file card index, arranged in alphabetical order by author name, giving publication details for each source in the appropriate format on a separate card. As you uncover new references you simply slot a new file card into the existing sequence, and at the final stage type directly from your cards to compose the bibliography. With the Harvard system, all you need to do in addition is to cite references at suitable points in the main text. With traditional footnotes, in addition to the bibliography file cards, you will need a list of numbered footnotes matching the sequence of number references in your text. It is particularly important to ensure that the two sets of numbers do not diverge when you have redrafted passages and added or deleted text or footnote material.

Producing Typescript

(a) **If your dissertation is the first occasion when you have produced a sizeable piece of typescript**, you should consider seriously learning to use a wordprocessing system on a micro-computer – so long as you can gain access to one at home or college. On a wordprocessor you can draft and redraft passages at the touch of a few keys, shorten or expand text, correct typing mistakes, order references automatically, and directly control the final appearance of your printed output. You can also give your teachers a presentable typescript from an early draft stage, increasing the likelihood of useful and extended feedback on your progress. By contrast, if you are using a typist you will only see your work in typed-up form in its very final stage, and before that must be content to operate with longhand versions – which are not as easy for you to assess or for your teachers to comment on.

(b) **If you are already keyboard literate** but have access only to a typewriter there may still be advantages in typing your own work. You do not have to write out all your material in quite the clean and legible form that another typist would require. For example, you can afford to go on operating with multiple bits of paper to be fitted into the finished text. During the typing itself you are able to make last-minute revisions and give a final polish to the prose. Typing your own material can also spare you the misunderstandings which a stranger to the material may make.

(c) **If you cannot type your dissertation at all**, writing it up in longhand and having it typed by someone else still entails some changes from ordinary essay writing. Write on lined paper of a standard size, using every other line (so that you can make insertions more easily), and on one side of the paper only (so that you can cut up pages and stick them back together in a different sequence, without having to rewrite material on the other side of the sheets). Your draft for the typist must be clear, with no risks of misunderstanding, an orderly sequence of material, and legible handwriting. When it is typed, check carefully for mistakes, making a log of where corrections are needed. If you are paying a typist do not accept assurances that mistakes are 'never' made: insist in advance that corrections are included in the initial price.

However you set about producing the typescript for your dissertation, check carefully that all aspects of the format you are using conform with any college regulations. If there are none, the following format will generally be appropriate: choose A4 paper, typed double-spaced on one side only, with a margin of around 3 cms on the left-hand side of the page (to allow for some form of binding), at least 1 cm on the right-hand side of the page, 3 cms space at the top and bottom of the page, a five-space indentation for starting new paragraphs, and pages numbered in a single sequence from the contents page onwards. Short quotations can be run on in the text within single quotation marks only (reserving double quotation marks for quotes within quotes). If a quotation is longer than about 30 words it should be set in from the side of the page by rather more than the paragraph indentation. You may want to use single spacing for indented quotes, footnote materials and the bibliography. But in all these cases there is usually no reason (apart from space-saving) why these materials should not be left in double spacing. Italics or emphases are indicated by underlining, unless you are using a word processor or electronic typewriter which can produce these types of script directly.

There are a few other basic conventions of publishing which it is useful to bear in mind. Always write in complete sentences, with a subject, verb and object. Never start a sentence with numeric figures: write 'Eighteen' not '18'. Do not use verbal abbreviations in the text (even such commonplace ones as & or

%). But abbreviations are legitimate for organizations or documents which are commonly initialized or referred to by acronyms in public debate (such as NATO or the BBC). Occasionally if you are citing very frequently from one or two major texts (for example, because you are discussing a single philosophical or literary work in great detail), it may be permissible to initialize or otherwise abbreviate the text reference, especially if you are using the Harvard system. In all dissertations, all abbreviations must be explained when they first appear, and should also be listed on a separate sheet immediately following the contents page and lists of tables and figures.

APPENDIX: REFERENCING SYSTEMS. FOOTNOTES, HARVARD SYSTEM AND BIBLIOGRAPHIES

Footnotes

Footnoting starts by including a small superscript number at the end of the sentence in which a quotation or other reference point is included. If possible, footnote numbers should not be included in mid-sentence: if several reference points fall within one sentence the distinctions between them can be clarified in the text of the footnote itself. A list of footnotes at the bottom of each page, or at the end of each chapter, or at the end of the dissertation as a whole then gives the referencing details in the form:

1. P. J. Dunleavy, *Studying for a Degree in the Humanities and Social Sciences* (London: Macmillan, 1986), pp. 11–12.

Notice that the publication details should include within brackets the place of publication, followed by a colon. Then as much of the publisher's name as is necessary to ensure distinctiveness (i.e. omitting initials, Ltd, Inc, etc.), followed by a comma, and then the year of publication.

If a particular source has been mentioned already the

reference details may be abbreviated by omitting the author's initials and publication details, as:

2. Dunleavy, *Studying for a Degree in the Humanities and Social Sciences*, p. 14.

If the book title itself can be shortened without losing meaning or distinctiveness, then this may be legitimate, as:

3. Dunleavy, *Studying for a Degree*, pp. 34–7.

For journal articles the first reference runs as follows:

4. P. J. Dunleavy, 'Bureaucrats, budgets and the growth of the state: reconstructing an instrumental model', *British Journal of Political Science*, vol. 15, no. 2 (1985), pp. 413–42.

Notice that in referencing article titles the use of capital letters is kept to the absolute minimum necessary. But in referencing book titles and journal names every major word starts with a capital letter. Journal names should always be given in full, but it is often permissible to give just the volume number of the journal before the date (i.e. leaving out the issue number). If this convention is followed the labels 'vol.', 'no.', and 'pp.' may be omitted, which for the example above gives just: 15, (1985), 413–42.

Subsequent references to journal articles can omit the author's initials, the subtitle of the paper (if there is one), the journal name, and the publication details, as:

5. Dunleavy, 'Bureaucrats, budgets and the growth of the state', p. 421.

If a book or article has several authors then the initial reference to it should give each author's name and initials in full. For a book or article with two authors, subsequent references should give both their last names, for example: Dunleavy and Ward. If there are three or more authors, subsequent references can simply give the first author's last name and add the abbreviation *et al.* (which signifies the latin 'et alia', meaning 'and others').

It is best to avoid using any other forms of abbreviations. The two most commonly employed are *ibid.* meaning 'the same reference as in the previous footnote', and *op. cit.* used in conjunction with an author's name to mean 'the same work as last cited for this author'. *Op. cit.* is particularly annoying for readers, who must then dredge back through previous footnotes to find the last occasion on which that author was cited before they have a clue which work is involved. There is less objection to *ibid.* if footnotes are arranged at the end of each chapter or of the dissertation. But in a sparsely referenced thesis with footnotes at the end of each page, *ibid.* can create similar problems to *op. cit.* in forcing readers to hunt back through earlier pages for information which should be instantly available.

Harvard Referencing

In Harvard referencing instead of entering a footnote number in the text, you place some basic reference material in brackets as follows (Dunleavy, 1986, pp. 234–7). Notice that what is included here is the author's last name, the year of publication of the source, and page numbers for the reference. If you are giving a general reference to a source then page numbers may not be strictly necessary, although in a dissertation they are usually desirable since examiners may be sceptical of vague referencing. It is better to use page numbers rather than chapter references, but the abbreviations Ch. or Chs can be employed if this is unavoidable. A semi-colon is used to separate several source citations in the same brackets, viz. (Dunleavy, 1986; Rowntree, 1973). To find out what these publication details refer to, the reader then turns directly to the bibliography, a comprehensive listing of all the references, arranged in alphabetical order. With Harvard referencing the bibliography must be entered in the modern format discussed in the next section.

Compared with traditional footnotes, the Harvard system has the very considerable advantage that there is no listing of references other than the bibliography itself: you do not have to type the source material details out twice. Nor do you have to worry about matching up footnote numbers in the text with numbers in a list of references, which makes it much easier to change text or references at different stages. To insert a new reference you just cite the new source in your text and add it to the bibliography. Consequently commercial publishers and most new journals have increasingly adopted the Harvard system in preference to footnotes.

The one serious disadvantage of the Harvard system is that the author names and dates inserted in brackets in the text can become obtrusive, especially if more than two or three sources are cited at any point. Some people also prefer footnotes because they allow them to add odd comments or asides which they do not want to include in the main text. The footnotes become a kind of subtext full of little digressions from the main argument. Harvard referencing discourages this practice, forcing you to decide whether a comment is really important (in which case it should be incorporated into the argument of the main text), or dispensable (in which case it can be left out altogether). But at dissertation level, even if a Harvard system is prescribed, there is generally no bar on having just a few footnotes – especially for any essential digressions (such as technical comments). One or two footnotes can be used to accommodate referencing to a large number of authors at one point: a footnote number is placed in the text and the note itself gives the publication details in the Harvard style. Such procedures should be used as little as possible, because they involve extra inconvenience to the reader, who first has to refer to the footnote and then look up the bibliography as well.

Bibliographies

A bibliography is a comprehensive list of all the materials cited in the work, basically arranged in the alphabetical order of the authors' names so that a reader can easily check which sources have been used. Obviously, a bibliography is indispensable in the Harvard system. By contrast, all the information it contains will already have been included in traditional footnotes, so that you may be tempted not to bother with this extra work. However, even if a bibliography is not absolutely required with footnotes, it is always desirable, since it is much easier for examiners to check what you have read without having to plod through all your footnotes.

Most items in bibliographies are 'secondary sources', that is, books and articles published by academic authors or other commentators. However, if your dissertation also involves consulting original documents, systematically reanalysing newspaper output over several years, or reading unpublished files, minutes or manuscripts, then all these are classified as 'primary sources'. They should be separately listed under this heading at the start of the bibliography. Similarly if published government statistics or survey data on computer tape have been reanalysed extensively in the research these should also be listed as primary sources. Within each section of the bibliography, alphabetical ordering of materials cited should be followed, but for primary sources (which often do not have an author as such) the first letters of the source title may be used for this purpose. There are two options for arranging normal secondary sources in bibliographies.

The modern bibliographical format *must* be used with the Harvard referencing system, and is preferable for use with traditional footnotes as well. In fact, you should always use this format unless your institutions' regulations prescribe otherwise. Information is presented as follows:

Dunleavy, P. J. (1985) 'Bureaucrats, budgets and the growth of the state: Reconstructing an instrumental model', *British Journal of Political Science*, vol. 15, no. iii, pp. 299–328.

Dunleavy, P. J. (1986) *Studying for a Degree in the Humanities and the Social Sciences* (London: Macmillan).

Notice that the sequence here is author last name, author initials, year of publication, book or article title, place of publication and publisher for a book; or journal name, volume (and issue) number, and pagination details for a paper. The advantages of this format are that it is easier to see the alphabetical progression of sources, since the author last name is the first piece of information presented. If several of an author's works are cited they are arranged by date of publication, the next item included after the author's initials. Multiple publications by the same author in the same year should be distinguished by adding a, b, c after the year date. Finally if a book or article is written by two or more authors, it is entered into the bibliography sequence by the surname of the first author. For any author, joint works are always entered after those which she has written alone. The bibliography should of course give full details of all authors for any work.

An alternative format for a bibliography presents the same information in virtually the same way as traditional footnotes, viz:

> P. J. Dunleavy, *Studying for a Degree in the Humanities and Social Sciences* (London: Macmillan, 1986).
> D. Rowntree, *Learn How to Study* (London: MacDonald, 1982).

This format does not provide bibliographical information very clearly. The reader has to scan past the author initials to reach the surname, and then retrieve the date from amongst the publication details. Similarly, the alphabetical sequence used for arranging references is less apparent than with the modern bibliography format above.

Summary of Suggestions: Writing Dissertations

1. Use techniques for generating information more systematically and extensively in conducting a documentation search; for example, scan recent journals comprehensively for articles or book reviews, or use on-line computer facilities to uncover possible new sources (p. 113).

2. With literature review dissertations, specify an angle of investigation at the outset. Look for elements in the existing literature which can be brought into an unusual conjunction, or different bodies of literature which might usefully be synthesized (for example, those of different countries, or different theoretical approaches, to a common topic) (p. 113).

3. With case-study dissertations, define a clear rationale for the applied work involved, and be clear what it is a case of. Look at academic case-studies and previous dissertations to get an idea of what may be feasible (p. 116).

4. Be cautious about adopting a focus-down model for a case-study dissertation. An opening-out approach may be easier to manage, and produce a closer connection between a case-study and broader academic themes (p. 117).

5. Write a dissertation synopsis as early as possible, and keep it under development until you begin writing a draft of the full text (p. 120).

6. Timetable your dissertation work carefully to avoid clashes with exam periods. Ration the time devoted to introductory work; if theory is overspecified before substantive research begins it may turn out to be inapplicable to later findings (p. 121).

7. Write up your findings as you go along, before you forget details, or 'overkill' the project and exceed word limits, or discover that you have chosen the wrong topic altogether (p. 123).

8. Allow at least a quarter of your available time for producing a final draft, plus two weeks for the mechanical operations of producing the typescript (p. 124).

9. Split a mini-dissertation of 5,000 words into around four sections. For a dissertation of 10 to 15,000 words use three to five chapters, subheadings, contents page, etc. Use enough organizers to give a clear structure to the text (p. 125).

10. Document literature sources and quotations carefully from the outset of your project, using either traditional footnotes or the Harvard referencing system, and a file card index to compose a bibliography (p. 125).

11. If you are not keyboard literate, consider learning how to use a wordprocessor to type your own dissertation. If you can use a typewriter this may still be preferable to having someone else type your work. If you pay someone, give them

a clean manuscript and insist that corrections are included in the cost (p. 127).

12. Check whether your college has regulations on the appearance of dissertations, and use a standard format if it does not. Observe basic publishing conventions (p. 128).

---

6   Revising for Exams

Reading Guide

Preparing for unseen written examinations draws on many
of the study skills already described, but also requires some
additional procedures. I examine:

1. Ways of beginning revision early on, and making sure
   that it is the right kind of revision.
2. The distinctive features of exam questions, and how to
   understand them.
3. The importance of undertaking 'active' revision, rather
   than passively memorizing materials.
4. The mechanics of writing up large numbers of practice
   essays or note answers.
5. Some common exam room problems.

For many students performance in written exams wholly
determines their degree result. Even those whose degrees are
assessed by a combination of methods usually find that
between a half and three-quarters of their marks are allocated
to examinations. The normal format of exam papers requires
students to answer three, four or five unseen questions within a
short period (usually 3 hours), without referring to books, notes
or other memory aids. Of course, there are some important
variations, such as 'open book' and 'take-away' papers. But the
traditional pattern of unseen written examinations still remains
a dominant form of assessment.

This phenomenon is hard to explain, since few educationists
doubt that traditional exams are a less than perfect assessment
system. People's performance can be quite markedly affected
by factors which have little to do with the objectives of higher
education, for example, the ability to handwrite essays at great
speed or to memorize large quantities of information. Exam

scripts are usually double- or triple-marked, but there are often considerable variations in the marks given by different examiners, or by the same examiners at different times. This indeterminancy is all the more important because in British universities and polytechnics the percentage point variation between a 'fail' script and one assigned a first-class mark is quite restricted (see below, p. 142). Written examinations also test only some kinds of abilities (such as writing short essays) and not others (such as undertaking research and developing a longer argument coherently).

Exams' popularity was originally associated with the late-nineteenth-century drive towards defining 'merit' (rather than patronage or wealth) as the criterion for academic success and entry to the professions. Examinations were valued for their impersonality and presumed objectivity. Written papers became the mainstay of public examinations partly to prevent various forms of cheating, collaboration, or corruption, and this concern continues to exercise universities and colleges. In addition written exams are relatively easy to administer, are familiar for staff and students to operate, and concentrate assessment into a short burst at the end of each academic year – a pattern which many teachers and some students find agreeable when compared with alternatives such as continuous or mid-year assessment.

Whatever their pros and cons, the most important feature of written exams is that they require specialized preparation, a revision and reorientation period which involves adapting your existing study skills to meet their particular requirements.

6.1 BEGINNING REVISION

Considering that each academic 'year' lasts barely nine months, a revision period of two or three months consumes quite a bit of your time. The onset of the exam-preparation season is publicly signalled by the winding-up of classes, dwindling attendance at lectures, and the permanent colonization of areas of the library previously only thinly populated. Revision classes attract attentive audiences if the teacher involved is perceived to have influence over the content of question papers. But all this is a transition phenomenon only, since most students do their core revision from home, retreating into a kind of purdah to grapple with their problems individually. This seclusion may have some pay-offs in terms of avoiding competitive pressures (such as implausible stories of night-long revision 'blitzes') or last-minute distractions (such as the knowledgeable tip about a 'dead cert' topic you have not revised). But as friends retreat into bed-sits all over town, it is important not to lead too hermit-like an existence, or to cut out necessary relaxation and social contacts.

However difficult you find it to 'get properly started' on revision, there are a number of relatively painless but time-consuming things worth doing as early as you can, say at the end of the Easter term or during that vacation.

(a) **Pick up copies of past examination papers** for the last three years. Earlier papers may be dated or relate to a previous version of your course or to topics now of less significance. Find out the precise timing of your examinations as early as you can, and sketch out a rough timetable of how you intend to deploy your time across subjects in the run-up to these dates.

(b) **Divide up your existing materials** – essays, class papers, lecture notes, and any notes from general reading – **into a number of topics of the kind asked about in the examination.** For each topic make a list of relevant questions from past exam papers, plus the topics discussed in your classes or tutorials, and relevant sections of course reading lists.

(c) **Decide how many topics you are going to tackle in your revision** and which these are going to be. Normally a whole-year course will include around 20 different class or lecture subjects, far more than you can cover in revision. You need a manageable number of topics, but including enough material to cover a reasonable range of questions. A useful rule of thumb is that you need to revise at least twice as many topics per paper as you are required to answer in the exam. In addition most exam papers contain one or two general questions (usually at the beginning or end) which are intended as fall-back questions for students in search of a last topic. With a bit of preparation these questions are often easier than they look, hence it is worth including one or two 'insurance' topics.

So if your exam rubric requires 4 questions you need a minimum of 4 × 2 basic topics, plus 1 'fall-back' topic in your revision. With 3 questions the topic list could fall to 7, while with 5 questions it rises to 11.

This rule of thumb can easily seem a tall order if you have not written many essays or class papers during a course, especially as it is important to emphasize that your revision topics should be clearly distinct from each other. Frequently there may be a mismatch between the division of materials used in class or tutorial questions and the kind of topics which are relevant for exam revision purposes. For example, foundation topics from the beginning of the year may be important in building up students' knowledge of a field, and yet rarely be examined. Hence it is important to check that your topics do not overlap each other, and that your final revision will not be overconcentrated in one area of the syllabus. For example, if the exam rubric requires you to answer at least one question in a particular part of the syllabus, the 2 × n rule implies that at least two of your revision topics should be in this area.

Trying to cover too many topics is just as futile a strategy as covering too few. If at the end of the day you are going to write four exam essays, there is absolutely no point in covering more than about 9–12 topics during revision. Beyond this level you will simply dissipate time and energy on acquiring information which you cannot conceivably use. If you cover too many topics in depth for one paper then you will overload your capacities to recall and organize information, possibly at the expense of performance in other papers as well. If you cover too many topics skimpily than you can easily fail to reach the level of writing and analysis required for useful degree marks.

In general, your revision topics should include those areas where you already have the most material, where you feel most confident of tackling the intellectual problems, or where your interest and motivation are higher. If you have written an essay or class paper on a topic then you are likely to have relevant books, photocopies of articles, and notes on your general reading, in addition to your earlier answer. Other topics to include are those where you have access to fellow students' materials, where your lecture notes are particularly clear or comprehensive, or where you can easily acquire new materials to cover the topic.

'Question spotting' is rather modestly useful in deciding what revision topics to settle on. The same question rarely comes up in identical formulations in exam papers two years running, so the last but one paper can often be more illuminating than the most recent. If a topic has increased in prominence or featured heavily in this year's reading lists or lectures by comparison with earlier papers, then this may be worth covering. But it is very rarely worth trying to include 'spotted' questions unless they also meet some of the criteria mentioned above, that is, unless you are going to be able to tackle them effectively.

(d) **Decide what additional basic materials are needed** for you to cover each topic effectively, and then set about acquiring them as early as you can. Because most revision is done at home, you must have a reasonable collection of books and articles available in each exam subject. If you delay too long in acquiring the necessary literature, a great deal of your later 'core' revision period may be absorbed in a last-minute chase after books. In the summer term, libraries tend to be emptied by the intensified demands of finals students, while bookshops' stocks are run down until the new academic year. If there is one key reading source for a topic, such as a book chapter or a paper, then find and photocopy it well in advance of the period when you are going to study it intensively. Similarly beg and borrow materials from fellow students long before the revision season starts, for then they will be harder to contact and more reluctant to part with anything in case it does not get returned. Lastly, remember that some sources of materials (such as public lending libraries) may require you to reserve books well in advance.

(e) **Get an idea of the broad range of marks you need to achieve.** There are a set of complicated and sensitive rules in each university and polytechnic (the 'examining conventions'), which determine the relationship between students' numerical marks and their class of degree. Because these rules are usually kept secret and vary widely, few generalizations about them are feasible. But out of eight final degree papers two common rules for awarding a particular class of degree are that (i) five papers reach the given level, or (ii) that four marks are at the class level, with two more only one class lower. In addition penalties usually attach to very poor marks in the remaining subjects, so they cannot be completely neglected.

British universities and polytechnics differ from American colleges in not making use of the full 100 per cent mark range. Usually degree grades and percentage marks translate as follows:

First class paper	70 per cent or over
Upper second paper	60–69 per cent
Lower second paper	50–59 per cent
Third class paper	40–49 per cent
Pass paper	34–40 per cent
Fail	Under 34 per cent

Hence the top three degree classes require:

Type of rule	'Best five papers'	'Four plus two'
First class degree	Five 70s	Four 70s and two 60s
Upper second degree	Five 60s	Four 60s and two 50s
Lower second degree	Five 50s	Four 50s and two 40s

Under these arrangements very small variations in exam marks can translate into different classes of paper and degree. Anomalies frequently occur. For example, consider two candidates with the following profiles of marks:

First candidate	75 71 65 58 58 57 56 55	Average: 62
Second candidate	63 63 62 61 55 52 48 46	Average: 56

The first candidate here has two first class papers, one upper second, and five lower second papers. Under the 'best five papers' or the '4 + 2' rules she cannot be awarded an upper second, and hence ends up with a 2.ii degree. The second candidate by contrast has four clear but low upper second papers, two lower second and two third class papers. Under the 'best five papers' rule she again gets a 2.ii. But under the '4 + 2' rule she gains an upper second degree, despite having a lower average mark than the first candidate! To some extent there is flexibility via the use of marginal percentage marks (such as 49, 59, and 69 in the mark scale above) for examiners' meetings to take into account each candidate's overall performance in fixing a paper's final marks. But no examiners' meeting has very much discretion in this respect, especially since marks have to be approved by visiting examiners from outside, whose role is partly to prevent any bending of the rules to fit individual candidates.

Because examining conventions are typically so byzantine, it is not worth trying to find out exactly what they are (although this seems a perfectly proper demand for students' unions to pursue). But do ask your tutor what you need to do in broad terms to achieve your target class of degree. For example, if a '4 + 2' rule operates this may imply dangers in overconcentrating on one or two papers at the expense of a wider range of good marks. By contrast, where quite different examining conventions apply (as at Oxford University) really exceptional marks in two or three subjects may be enough to secure a first class degree.

There are three general lessons to draw from this brief digression into examining conventions. First, since a 3 per cent variation in your marks on one paper could be decisive for your class of degree, it is vitally important to make each exam script look as competent, as organized and as finished as you possibly can. Do not ignore potentially useful suggestions because they will only marginally alter your marks. In borderline cases the margin may be critical. Similarly, never despair of improving your exam performance. However late you begin your revision, however much you may feel that you have not worked during the year, even a short period of concentrated revision and exam preparation will almost certainly produce a considerable improvement in the marks you eventually receive.

Second, as a general rule it is no good trying to 'fine-tune' your revision efforts in line with the detailed marks you expect to get in different papers. Because such tiny differences in percentage terms separate one class of paper from another, and because most examining conventions require evidence of some 'strength' in over two-thirds of your final papers, probably the best rule of thumb is to put equal effort into every paper. Certainly you can never afford to let any paper slide completely. For example, in some institutions, a single third class mark might prevent an otherwise high-scoring candidate being awarded first class honours.

Third, do not approach unseen written exams convinced that they will accurately or objectively measure your knowledge, intellectual capabilities or work done on a course. This kind of thinking translates every personal deficiency and missed study opportunity into an exam liability. Instead you should recognize that exams are a highly imperfect assessment system in which small differences in performance are often magnified out of all recognition. Consequently the only sensible approach to take is a fairly cynical, instrumental one. Underperformance in examinations usually indicates only that you need more practice in doing exams, rather than anything fundamental about your intellectual, academic or personal qualities.

The suggestions made here are useful preliminary steps to take before you get down to revision proper. They do not require you to spend hours slogging over books or to face up to any fundamental intellectual difficulties you may have. In this sense they could seem like the displacement activities we all use to put off doing something unpleasant. However, so long as they are undertaken well in advance, they are an important and necessary foundation for a more concentrated burst of revision closer to the exams themselves, when it will be most useful.

6.2 UNDERSTANDING EXAM PAPERS

Virtually all degree examinations are set directly by the teachers involved in each course. Lecturers are much more directly involved in examining than schoolteachers, who work to a syllabus and question papers set by a remote public exam board, and who do not usually get to see the final scripts produced by their students. Since nobody stands to gain by running a course where students do badly, there is an obvious need for universities and polytechnics to regulate the sorts of exam papers which are set. All papers are originated by at least two lecturers. On compulsory papers or first-year courses with many classes, a large group of teachers may be involved in preparing the draft question paper. Each academic department then has a special meeting to consider all the drafts of exam papers for which it is responsible, to check their clarity and level of difficulty. Finally, all universities and polytechnics must appoint external examiners from other institutions, who also approve question papers and maintain correct standards of difficulty.

These complicated arrangements, and teachers' direct involvement in setting questions and marking scripts, both contribute to the considerable importance of examinations in academic life. And, of course, teachers in higher education are almost always people who have done well at these examinations in the past, who therefore tend to see them as significant in terms of their own personal development. With this kind of background underlying their production, it is worth taking examination questions seriously as an art form in their own right. Although students often profess themselves puzzled by 'stupid' or 'obvious' questions, these first impressions are rarely accurate. Most unseen exam questions have the following characteristics.

(a) **They are very condensed, almost epigrammatic** in character. Traditional approaches to higher education place a premium on asking very short, one- or two-line questions, producing very 'spare' examination papers.

(b) **They tend to be deliberately simple-looking questions**, which contain few specific hints about the level of answer expected. Similar questions can be asked on different exam papers falling within one discipline, but with quite different kinds of answer being expected. There is also something of a mythology in more literary humanities and social sciences that 'the same questions' can be asked at different levels of exam (for example, first-year, finals or masters' levels), but that the answers expected at each level will differ radically.

(c) **Questions use chiefly an 'ordinary language' vocabulary**, with technical terms kept to the minimum necessary to define the question precisely. Many exam questions express theoretical viewpoints without explicitly labelling them. At degree level, 'Write all you know about X' questions are rare, because they could simply trigger an automatic unravelling of memorized materials in much the same form that they were learnt. Most exam questions are less direct, requiring you to recognize the substantive controversies being referred to, and then adapt your material to deal with a new formulation of basically quite familiar problems.

A couple of examples may be useful at this point:

> 'If I look out of the window, I can see that it is cold outside.' Is there anything loose or inaccurate about this way of speaking?

This simple-looking question, taken from a third-year General Philosophy paper at Oxford University, is actually about the 'sense-data transfer' controversy in the theory of knowledge. It asks when it is legitimate to infer from the existence of one sense's stimuli (such as visual perceptions of frost, icy puddles, snow) to the presence of others (such as feeling cold). Or consider the enquiry:

> What are the prerequisites of democracy?

This third-year political science question might have come from a paper on comparative political institutions – in which case an appropriate answer might discuss the level of social and economic development in a country, the mechanisms for conducting fair elections, the presence of an independent judiciary, the freedom of the press, and so on. In fact the question is drawn from a political philosophy paper, so that a relevant response would be expected to focus chiefly on the concept of democracy, and its relation with the ideas of majority rule, a 'popular will' or the protection of civil liberties. Hence the same question asked in the context of two differing exams would be expected to elicit quite different styles of answer.

(d) Because exam questions are very condensed, deliberately literary and rely on ordinary language, **they accentuate a fundamental difficulty with unseen written exams –**

finding the right starting level for your answers. Many people blow large amounts of marks by writing scripts at a level which is simply too basic to be useful in gaining marks. Writing 'textbook' answers (often in response to the most 'straightforward' looking questions) is an apparently risk-minimizing strategy which people often adopt at school. But considering how little time per question is allowed in most written exams, this is a disastrous habit to carry into finals. Your central task in unseen exams is to show off the maximum amount of high-level knowledge in an organized way relevant to the question asked, in an essay of perhaps four sides of A4 paper. Any portion of this space or of the tiny amount of time available (usually 45 minutes or an hour per question) which is wasted on writing out basic materials that could be taken as read is therefore very serious. The fact that what is written in a script is 100 per cent 'right', in that it contains no factual or argumentative errors, is often quite irrelevant.

An analogy may help here. Assume that you are walking over to your car with the person who is to give you your first driving test. You are unlikely to improve the examiner's confidence in your skills on the road by explaining that the car has four wheels, an internal combustion engine, a steering wheel, brakes, and so on. Although everything you say is absolutely correct, it is just inappropriate to bring up such basic information in this context. The driving test examiner will assume that you knew all this long before you started guiding several tons of steel at lethal speeds along the highway.

There are two useful steps to take early on in your revision to make sure that you have thoroughly familiarized yourself with your exam papers.

(i) **Decide the style of answer which is appropriate to each paper.** Look at how the questions asked relate to the syllabus, the lecture content, and the class or essay topics which you encountered during the year. Each paper should have a distinctive 'feel' for you, particularly where you are doing a large number of papers at once. Often people have most difficulty in finding a style on their weakest papers, which they approach in the style of papers where they feel more confident.

Do not expect an exact match, however, between question papers, syllabus, and course content. Syllabuses are often slightly anachronistic, as teachers introduce topics not obvious in the formal syllabus and de-emphasize others which are mentioned. Similarly, remember that lecture series often include large sections designed to get beginning students up to scratch or to fill in a background: these materials rarely feature in the end-of-year examinations. Finally, on large courses taught by several class teachers, you may need to check that the topics which you have covered in your classes do normally feature in the question papers. Occasionally class teachers who are not also examiners cover issues which are rather unlikely to be exam topics.

(ii) **Clarify at what level your answers should be pitched.** Try and decide what knowledge past exam papers already take as read. If the questions look the same as those which you have already tackled at a lower level of examination (for example, first-year questions resemble those completed at 'A' level) be especially careful to ensure that your revision answers have some extra ingredients or improvements. It is particularly easy to 'undershoot' the required standard in degree exams by pitching your answer at too low a level, especially one appropriate for an earlier set of examinations. Try to picture the audience for your essay: what are the examiners looking for? Do your answers include material so basic that any rational examiner would assume you knew it anyway, and which is consequently unlikely to attract any extra marks? And bear in mind when determining the appropriate level of analysis that your writing time will be very severely restricted.

6.3 DOING ACTIVE REVISION

Many students seem to assume that the best way of preparing for exams is a dedicated attempt to cram in as much knowledge as they can. They become convinced that they know far too little material to do themselves justice in the exams. Consequently revision is a time for 'mugging up' masses of new material, especially work they missed doing earlier in the course. The key activities of the revision period should be reading, and making notes on material read. Revision should be a great slog, accomplished by as many hours work a day as possible.

Even people who completely accept that active learning methods are most appropriate for their ordinary work still seem to believe that passive cramming is the only way of preparing for written exams. Unseen exams can encourage a dread of 'getting things wrong', or a morbid 'fear of forgetting' material which you have already learnt. This can lead to an overemphasis on simple mnemonics and repetitive learning even of familiar literature. Previous experiences of revising for public exams at school can be a misleading guide here. At degree level, exams are much less straightforward, and the assessment system places a premium on your producing coherent, organized answers at a high level. These problems are often complicated by people's unwillingness to relate their study habits in an open-minded way to what will actually be required of them in their papers. Because exams are far more intimidating than ordinary study activities, people often find it nerve-wracking to look constructively at alternative ways of preparing for them.

By contrast my advice reflects three convictions.

1. **Exams test mainly whether you've practised doing exams.** They are very specialized and untypical academic occasions. Outstanding exam performances may reflect intellectual distinction quite sensitively. But for most people, exam scripts are rather a poor guide to how much they have understood or learnt in a whole course. Instead your performance will reflect in large part how much you have practised writing very short answers to specific exam questions. At a very late stage in a course there is no point in trying to understand new material or make great intellectual advances unless they can be directly useful in producing better exam scripts.

2. **Managing overload is the key exam problem.** Most people who do badly in exams know far more course material than is necessary to write good exam answers. People fail to do themselves justice not through ignorance but because they have learnt far more than they can remember or write down

under exam conditions. There is so much which they could write that they do not know where to start, or how to organize their material. If they have not thought explicitly about the problems of responding to a question at the right level, their essays often begin as doomed attempts to 'rewrite the textbook' – only to finish up as rushed (and hence garbled) efforts to answer more relevantly before time runs out. Despite much advice to the contrary, relatively few people seriously practise how to write out answers briefly and clearly, how to select the key arguments and facts, and how to leave out the less important, more basic or irrelevant material. But the exam room is the very last place to start trying to come to terms with these problems for the first time.

3. **Active revision is quicker and more efficient than passive cramming.** Revision and (perhaps) exam performance can both be improved with a few weeks work if they are done more effectively. Passive revision, reading other people's thoughts and trying to memorize as much as possible, is unnecessarily difficult and time-consuming. It is also quite general revision, trying to master a particular book, article or set of lecture notes, rather than being directed to specific exam questions. By contrast, efficient preparation for exams should be active revision, requiring you to think on your own while you try to master topics. It should be specifically tied to exam questions, so that you can practise unravelling what questions mean and adapting your existing knowledge to fit in with what is asked. The key activities of the revision period should be writing, and sorting out your own ideas. Active and topic-focused revision need not take hours of slog because you learn much faster, and you will not forget information as easily. In addition the more active revision you do, the greater the stock of revision materials which you will build up. And the key element in accomplishing all this is to write plenty of practice answers.

Types of Practice Answers

All practice answers are framed in response to a specific question, usually taken from a recent past exam. There are three different approaches, each of which is appropriate to particular people, kinds of exam, or stages of revision.

1. **Full answers** involve working through a question, taking however long is needed to formulate a satisfactory answer. In many technical fields (such as computing, accounting, econometrics, statistics or linguistics) this approach may be the only way of understanding what past exam questions mean and how they can be answered. For example, in technical economics a mathematical problem requires you to work through the calculations involved, checking at the end with the textbooks to ensure that you have used formulae correctly. Somewhat similarly, translating a passage of text in Anglo-Saxon or a foreign language is an activity for which there are no shortcuts; again after finishing you will need to be sure that each element of the translation was correctly carried out. Finally, if you have done no work at all in a non-technical subject it may be necessary to write up full answers during the revision period, simply in an attempt to catch up on essays which you did not complete during normal coursework.

2. **Timed essays** are trial answers written under full exam conditions, that is, responding to a question from a past paper, without referring to books or notes, and sticking closely to the time allowed. In all subjects where you have to write essays in exams this approach is very valuable in making you realize just how much (or how little) you can write down in 45 minutes or an hour. It shows how your arguments and writing style perform under pressure, and gives you a first-hand impression of what it will be like to answer questions in that subject under exam conditions. It also allows you to identify and correct numerous minor failings, such as bad spelling, poor style, illegible hand-writing, or a tendency to repeat the question phrasing hypnotically.

However, timed essays also have some disadvantages. What you can scribble down in 45 minutes when you are just revising will usually be less than you can achieve in the more pressurized atmosphere of the exam room, so you may discourage yourself unnecessarily. Most people also spend a long time nerving themselves up to write out answers under exam conditions, and complete only one or two per paper. Unless you can do them very quickly timed essays will not be an effective general approach to basic revision.

3. **Note answers** are again responses to a specific exam question, but this time written out only in note form. In all essay-based exams their advantages are considerable. First, because they are not continuous text, it is easier for you to see the basic plan of your answer, and to try to improve the structure of your argument. Second, because your answers are in the form of notes they are much easier to re-read later, rearrange, and revise from. Third, note answers are much quicker and easier to do. With a bit of practice you should be able to complete a note answer from start to finish in about an hour to two hours. Hence you can cover far more topics and practise tackling more exam questions, making this a very effective way to undertake active bread-and-butter revision. Fourth, note answers are often better than timed essays at showing you what you can do at your best.

If you will be sitting essay-based exams, try writing out two or three timed essays and note answers as early as you can in your revision period, to see how you get on with both. Since exams allow you very little space to show off your knowledge of course materials, a crucial requirement of the revision period is that you practise writing tightly organized answers, jam-packed with the sorts of points which earn exam marks. If you can do this by writing lots of timed essays, sufficient to cover the number of topics you need in each subject, then so much the better. But doing large numbers of note answers is an alternative way of proceeding which is more realistic for most students.

Producing Practice Answers

It is easy enough to advise someone 'Do your revision by writing up a lot of practice answers'. But how exactly should you set about it? If you have decided to write a full answer or a timed essay, your approach may be quite similar to normal essay-writing (pp. 83). However, exam answers are typically much shorter than mid-year essays. They need to be simply structured, easier to write out quickly, tightly organized, and much more selective in the material included. By contrast, note answers are clearly a different mode of proceeding from normal coursework.

To start a practice answer, take a topic that you are beginning to revise and read over the relevant materials in textbooks or your files. Select a question from a recent past exam paper. Do not wait till you know the topic inside out before formulating a response. Instead tackle the question fairly 'cold', before you have spent a great deal of time working in the area. A practice answer is most effective as a revision aid in pinpointing what you do not know already, so that you can give it special attention. Formulating a response is easier if you take it in separate stages. I suggest the following phases: generating ideas; analysing the question; defining a response; organizing and writing the answer; reassessment; and adding new materials. After some practice, you might be able to complete the first five stages for a revision note answer in around 15 minutes each. Obviously the last stage of reading and noting additional material will take as long as you need.

Stage 1: Generating ideas

Have you ever started an exam question on which you were supposed to write for 40 minutes, but then run out of ideas half way through the time? Yet as soon as you leave the exam room, you can think of five or six important things which you knew all along but could not recall? Just as in normal essay-writing, this over-restrictive focus reflects a failure to 'surface' all the ideas which may be relevant to the question right at the start. It is far easier in exams to become hypnotized by one possible response to a question, so that you lose track of alternative arguments or lines of attack. To make sure you do not reject material too quickly, set aside a few minutes of each revision answer as a brainstorming session. Here you jot down any idea you have about the question, without being critical about its exact relevance at this stage. Jot things down quickly and in any order that they occur to you. Then link up ideas with arrows or boxes. Here is a checklist of ingredients you might look for in almost any kind of answer.

(i) **Concepts** – the question itself almost always contains some key terms, but are there any hidden ideas as well?

(ii) **Debates** – most exam questions in the humanities and social sciences relate to controversies – whether conflicts of big theories, or empirical disagreements. If you cannot see two or more possible viewpoints, look again.

(iii) **Values and style** – can be as important in differentiating viewpoints in arts subjects as explicit theoretical approaches in the social sciences. What are the key ideals or themes which are involved in the topic?

(iv) **Proofs** – in more technical subjects, there may be key diagrams, formulae or graphs which need careful presentation. What conditions do these proofs assume, and are there any problems, limitations or anomalies in their operation?

(v) **Evidence** – what kind of empirical or applied information is relevant? Remember this could include examples, quotations, text analysis, statistics (not whole tables), case-studies, surveys, less systematic evidence (for example, official reports, impressions, and so on).

(vi) **Authors** – who are the big names in the field, associated with concepts, debates or evidence? Remember, you need key names only, not obscure authors on obvious points.

Stage 2: Analysing the question

One of the most important things to practise during revision is how to quickly take exam questions apart until you understand them inside out. At this stage you are not hunting for concept definitions to put directly into your essay, you are simply trying to understand the question for your own benefit.

(i) **Identify all the problem words in the question.** Look not just at the big flashy concepts, but also at the little words that string them together. Look for the 'command' words as well: is the question asking for description, evaluation, explanation, analysis, comparison, discussion or what?

(ii) **Analyse the major concepts carefully.** Follow the procedures in Chapter 3. Look for the concept's synonyms, partner words, universe, antonyms, antonyms of antonyms, and different forms. But remember that only a small part of this information may need to be explicitly incorporated in the answer. The idea is to stop you misconstruing past exam questions during revision, not to encourage you to spend precious time in the actual exam on defining all the concepts implied in a question. Be *very* parsimonious in deciding which concepts will need formal definition in your answer, and try to make these as precise and succinct as you can.

(iii) **Rewrite each question you tackle in your own words.** As with ordinary essays, 'translate' the question without using any of the original terms. Applied consistently this rule of thumb forces you to examine every part of the question you are answering, and to consider a range of possible meanings for each term and for the question as a whole. Because exam questions are often condensed and epigrammatic a two-line question may take up eight or ten lines in its fully rewritten form. And as I noted above, decoding exam questions often means reading theoretical concepts or controversies into an ordinary language question. Watch for open-ended questions (pp. 85–6) and interpret them in a manageable form. In revision try to identify explicitly any distracting opportunities for wandering off the point, so that you can better avoid them in the exam. Finally, be especially careful not to incessantly repeat phrases or concepts from the past exam question hypnotically in an attempt to demonstrate relevance: as with ordinary essays, the repeated element is often the least analysed part of the question (p. 83).

(iv) **Eliminate any irrelevant ideas generated at the previous stage.** Once you have fully understood the question, go through your ideas sheet and eliminate any entries which are not relevant. You will almost invariably have some jottings which on reflection you now feel should be deleted. Now is the time to scrub them, rather than wasting time trying unavailingly to integrate them into an otherwise coherent practice answer.

Stage 3: Defining the type of answer

Many people start exam answers with long 'I'm just getting my head together' introductions while they try to sort out their ideas. This trait is not fatal in normal essays or assignments because they are open-ended. If the introduction consumes more space, the overall length of the answer simply increases to compensate. But in exams, writing space and time wasted in orientating yourself is simply lost to you. It cannot be made up elsewhere, except by over-running your time on that question, which almost always implies a greater loss of marks on a later answer in the paper. Normally, lengthy introductions reflect the difficulty of reacting to a question on a familiar topic which is nonetheless asked from a different or unexpected angle. During your revision, practice answers should help you to become expert at adapting your existing material so that it can quickly and directly address a variety of new questions. Three steps are useful in defining an appropriate response.

(i) **Designate an explicit starting level appropriate for the question.** What material would be too basic or obvious to include? Are there 'confuser' themes or interpretations of the question which it is important to avoid?

(ii) **Decide whether your answer will be organized as a descriptive, analytic or argumentative essay** (pp. 86–95). Remember that narrative or chronological answers, 'guidebook' or 'textbook' responses, as well as essays organized around a random sequence of authors are all classed as 'descriptive' essays. Since exam answers are extremely short, the disadvantages of descriptive patterns of essay organization are greatly reinforced. Descriptive essays tend to look disorganized. They require a great many 'facts' or other materials, otherwise answers can look crude. They typically encourage you to start an answer at too basic a level. Lastly a descriptive pattern of essay organization cannot suggest useful criteria for selecting small amounts of relevant, high-level material. For all these reasons, I would suggest that analytic or argumentative essays are preferable forms for most essay-based exam answers to follow.

(iii) If you do adopt an argumentative or analytic structure, remember that under exam conditions **good labels, and necessary 'jargon' or technical language, are short-cut devices** which can save you a lot of time. Good labels show that you understand the field, and particularly help to prevent what you write seeming too closely derived from the literature.

Stage 4: Organizing and writing the answer

So far all you have got is a list of ideas, a clear notion of what the question asks, and a general picture of how you will respond. Now you have to define the detailed structure of the answer. In unseen exams you can only write short answers so the main organizing device is the paragraph, although headings are perfectly legitimate if you wish to use them. Examiners are looking for evidence of well-organized thought and pay a lot of attention to paragraph openings in indicating the plan of your answer. Three key steps are involved in organizing a note answer.

(i) **Split your answer materials into between four and eight paragraphs.** In 45 minutes or an hour you will not write more than a few sides of paper, so eight paragraphs will be about maximum, four about a minimum for a well-structured answer. To decide what should go where, take a couple of sheets of paper and physically split them up into boxes for each paragraph. Write out an informative heading for each box and number it. Ask yourself why paragraph 1 comes before 2 and 3, rather than in some other sequence. Try and make sure that the core material in your answer is dealt with at the front or in the middle of your essay. Do not leave all the good points to the end, because you will be writing under severe time pressure, and therefore the end of your essay can often get garbled or rushed. Make sure your paragraph headings do not overlap, that they clearly do different things, that the essay builds up an argument as it progresses, and that it does not go round in circles.

(ii) **Transfer all the items on your ideas sheet into one or other of the paragraph boxes** – go through each idea seeing where it should fit into your paragraph structure. Check that one paragraph is not getting too full up – if it is, split it into two and run together two of the smaller paragraphs. Try to get a logical structure to the sequence of ideas *within* each paragraph as well as between paragraphs.

(iii) **Write down enough material on each point in your argument.** For full answers, write as much as you need to master the topic. For timed essays, how much you write is obviously determined by the available time. For note answers, remember that what you write both provides you with practice at focusing on exam questions and generates notes for you to use in subsequent revision. Make sure that the notes for each paragraph do not become fully fledged text because then you may lose your grip on the overall plan. But remember that when you look at a note answer again some weeks later, you should not have to try and decipher a series of cryptic jottings.

Stage 5: Reassessment

In order to get most benefit from your revision answers, you need to be critical about them. If you can get friends or your tutor to look at some of your answers their reactions will always be useful. You can do a great deal to improve your own work, however, simply by having a separate stage in your revision where you sit back and appraise how your answer looks so far.

(i) **For full answers**, check whether you could realistically hope to reproduce what you have written under exam conditions. If the material looks hard to remember, is this because your answer is still written in other people's terms? If the answer is too long, how could you condense or edit the materials involved?

(ii) **For note answers**, check the feasibility of your plan. For example, count the number of ideas you have got in the plan. Obviously getting across fifty ideas in 40 minutes is not going to be easy. Equally too few ideas may leave you repeating yourself. Could your argument be simplified and made easier to remember and reproduce under pressure? Try writing out difficult passages in full. Some parts of any note answer may need to be written out in full, including:

> complicated definitions;
> explaining key proofs, diagrams or arguments in theoretical subjects;
> brief summaries of major theoretical positions;
> brief accounts of case-studies, where the salient material is presented without being obscured by incidentals;
> snappy references to examples or evidence.

The basic rule is: if you look at any part of a note answer and feel uneasy about how you would implement it under exam conditions, try writing out that passage as finished text.

(iii) **For timed essays**, questions about the practicability of the answer are less important, assuming that you have stuck to the time limit. But check how relevant your answer is and whether it includes the most salient points. Try to identify the things which go wrong in your writing under presure, looking especially for repetitions, woffle, vagueness, or mannerisms which detract from the answer's effectiveness.

(iv) **For all types of answer**, check that your first paragraph is not just padding, and that you get into the core argument as quickly as possible. Because of time constraints, exam answers should be much more 'front-loaded' than ordinary tutorial or class essays. That is, the core material and central arguments must be dealt with in the beginning and middle of your plan (rather than coming more towards the end as in most normal essay plans). If less crucial material is placed at the end of an exam answer, then you can develop it if you have time but summarize drastically if you are being squeezed. Check that however pressed for time you may be, you will be able to insert a short overall conclusion to bring different threads of the argument together.

Stage 6: Adding new material

Once you have an initial answer to an exam question, you can begin checking through your texts, essays and earlier notes, to see if anything has been left out which should be included. It should be easier to absorb new material effectively, because your answer provides you with a record of what you already know. Consequently you need only to look through your sources to try to identify new usable material, that is, ideas or evidence which you can directly incorporate into your practice answer. Do not be distracted by the elegance with which other authors make a point: concentrate on asking 'Is there anything different here which I could use?'.

Adding new material is easiest when you are doing note answers. Simply write amendments and additions on to your plan in a different colour ink, or add on new sheets to the answer. In this way you will get a clear record of what you tend to forget, as well as what you remember. With timed essays or full answers, small additions and corrections can be handled in the same way. For more extensive revisions, you need to summarize the new materials in your own words, using scissors and paste to edit them into your existing text at appropriate points.

6.4 TAKING EXAMS

Apart from effective revision, there are no great secrets involved in doing yourself full justice in the examination itself.

Nonetheless three key commonsense points are often ignored.

(a) **Stick religiously to the exam rubric**, ensuring that you allocate your time evenly between the required number of answers. I noted above (pp. 142–3) the idiosyncratic marking schemes used by examiners in higher education, especially the restricted mark range between a pass level around 34 per cent and a first class degree level of 70 per cent plus. This pattern of marking implies that while it is relatively easy to earn the first twenty or thirty percentage points on an answer, however brief, it becomes progressively more difficult to gain further marks as you move up the scale (see Figure 6.1 for a hypothetical example).

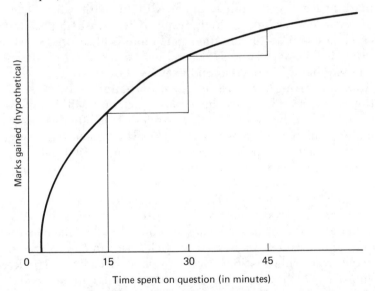

Figure 6.1: The diminishing returns on time spent per question

The implications of these diminishing returns to time expended are quite simple. If you prolong the period spent on one of your answers at the expense of producing a very rushed or abbreviated final answer, then you will almost inevitably gain far fewer marks on your overlengthened answer than you lose on the later botched question. This is even more true of the common situation where people spend so much time on their first answer that they fail to write anything at all on their last required answer. Consider the following numerical example. A student decides to spend twice the time allowed on her first answer so as to boost the marks she receives – and succeeds in pushing up the mark from an upper second 65 to a first class 71. She gets safe upper second marks of 63 and 62 on two further questions, but has no time to write anything at all on a fourth required question. The calculation of her overall grade on the paper is therefore: 71 + 63 + 62 = 196 marks total for the paper. But divided by the 4 questions required, this gives an average of only 49, a mark which is borderline between a third class and a lower second degree. Now it is very likely that the examiners in this case will exercise judgement so as to award a mark at least in the fifties, but it is problematic whether an upper second would definitely result. By contrast suppose the candidate kept to the question time limits and secured marks instead of 65, 63, 62 and 51. Here a total mark of 241 produces an unambiguous upper second average of over 60.

(b) **Scan through the whole question paper at the start of the exam**, marking those questions which you will definitely attempt, and those which are 'possibles'. It is often useful in understanding one question to know what other topics are covered by the exam. Very few examiners let substantially the same question slip on to the paper in different forms of wording. So if two questions look very similar, then you are almost certainly misreading one of them. On the other hand, looking at the remaining exam questions may also help to remind you of materials relevant to your chosen topics. Finally, since exam questions are often not immediately clear, it can be very useful to let your subconscious work away at decoding a tricky question which you will have to attempt later in the exam, while you first tackle a more straightforward answer.

(c) **Briefly plan each of your answers just before you start writing.** The whole point of developing your skills in writing note answers or timed essays is to enable you almost automatically to debug the question, spot any problems involved (such as open-ended questions), identify key concepts or terms, and produce a very quick sketch outline of your answer. One or two minutes spent jotting ideas down on scrap paper can avoid your misunderstanding the question or recalling relevant material only when already half way through an answer. Planning your answer should prevent 'false starts' where you write a promising couple of paragraphs, only to dry up after 20 minutes, by which time it is usually too late to begin an alternative answer. A quick run through the mental checklist of concepts, controversies, examples, proofs and authors can also prevent you veering off into theoretical vagueness where an empirical reference is required, or operating with purely descriptive materials unstructured by theoretical ideas. But do not underestimate the difficulties of sketching even the briefest essay plan in the rather frantic atmosphere of an exam room. Your fellow candidates will all seem to have covered pages of handwriting by the time your three or four minutes of planning time are finished. Unless you have some standard procedures for tackling questions, you will find it hard to write in an organized way under these trying conditions.

Summary of Suggestions: Revising for Exams

1. Begin revision early by picking up copies of past exam papers, and identifying at least twice as many topics to tackle as you have to answer questions in the exam. Collect missing materials you need for each topic. And find out what general kinds of marks you need to achieve to reach your target degree (p. 139).

2. Do not try to 'fine tune' the revision effort you put into your papers, since very small percentage mark differences separate one class of answer from another. Do not let any paper slide completely. The best rule may be to put equal effort into all your papers (p. 139).

3. Take exam questions seriously as an art form, and thoroughly familiarize yourself with the ways in which examiners phrase questions in your subjects (p. 145).

4. Fix the style of answer appropriate to each of your papers,

and clarify at what starting level your answers should be pitched. Be careful not to undershoot the required standard by reproducing basic material which could be taken as read, or by answering in a manner appropriate for a lower level of examination (p. 146).

5. Use active methods of revision, emphasizing a lot of practice answers, because exams test mainly how much you have practised doing exams. Managing overload is the key exam problem; and active revision is quicker and more effective than passive cramming (p. 149).

6. Write practice answers as full answers during revision in any technical exams, and perhaps if you badly need to catch up on a completely neglected subject (p. 151).

7. Write at least a few timed essays for any essay-based exam, to see how much or how little you can scribble down in the time available. But be aware that you may perform better in a real exam than under 'artificial' exam conditions (p. 151).

8. Use note answers to get a clearer idea of how you are planning your answers; to quickly create a set of revision notes; to cover more topics; and to get a better idea of what you may be able to do at your best (p.152).

9. Tackle practice answers fairly 'cold', rather than waiting until you know the topic inside out (p. 153).

10. To generate ideas for a practice answer, use a checklist of concepts, debates, values and style, proofs, evidence, and authors (p. 154).

11. To understand exam questions during revision, identify all the problem words, analyse the major concepts using techniques from Chapter 3, and rewrite the question in your own words. In writing a practice answer, be parsimonious about including definitional material; and delete at this point any irrelevant material from your generating ideas stage (p. 154).

12. To define an answer, designate an explicit starting level, and decide whether an essay answer will be organized on descriptive, analytic or argumentative lines (p. 156).

13. To organize and write the answer, think up between four and eight informative paragraph headings; transfer all your ideas into one of these boxes; and write down enough material to clarify the argument at each point (p. 157).

14. Reassess full answers or note answers to check their practicability under exam conditions. Reassess timed essays to see how your writing behaves under pressure (p. 158).

15. Check that any practice answer is 'front-loaded', that the introduction is not padded, and that material at the end can be appropriately 'concertina-ed' under pressure (p. 159).

16. Add new material on to your practice answers, using it as the baseline for quick, interrogative reading (p. 160).

17. Always answer the required number of questions in any exam, and be aware of the diminishing returns on time spent per question (p. 161).

18. In the exam room, read the whole question paper carefully at the start. To avoid 'false starts', briefly plan each answer (using the checklist in suggestion 10 above) before you begin writing (p. 162).

7 Turning Study Skills into Life Skills

Reading Guide

Two aspects of the relationship between studying in higher education and subsequent career experiences are explored:

1. The extent to which degree-level education can help people develop career skills in solving problems, working in committees, writing reports and mounting oral presentations.
2. Some key differences between life as a student and most work environments, such as working in large organizations, or developing institutional 'know-how'. Some career demands entail expanding your personal capacities, while others imply a narrowing of your interests and capabilities.

Studying for a degree often immediately precedes a crucial period of making career choices. Higher education institutions play a key role in switching people into different career paths, even though there are rather low correlations between academic performance and career success (at least measured in terms of job advancement or level of income attained). In most of the humanities and the social sciences, relatively few students directly use more than a fraction of the knowledge gained during their academic courses in their career work. Yet virtually everyone uses some of the study skills or methods of working developed in this period. And for many people, the 'deep structure' of their degree subject or higher education institution – the values, concepts and methods of working which underlay courses and teaching – may exert a considerable lasting influence on their approach to career tasks.

Of course, academic work is not the only way in which students become orientated towards later careers. For some privileged students a degree is only a necessary condition for entering a career already marked out by family connections. Non-academic opportunities in higher education can also be of crucial importance in aiding people to break into a particular career path. For example, experience in student journalism is probably more useful than most non-applied coursework if you want to work in the mass media. In many areas of business management, education, and the public sector, one-year graduate courses serve to bridge the gap between general first degrees and specific careers. In addition, established professions such as law, accounting, and higher education teaching impose lengthier qualification periods which greatly determine peoples' later career development. However, the grounds for emphasizing study skills and approaches acquired on first-degree courses remain substantial. Post-graduate or professional education is still a minority pursuit, and in many cases whether people gain access to these courses is conditioned by their performance at first-degree level.

7.1 ACQUIRING CAREER SKILLS IN HIGHER EDUCATION

Some career skills can be greatly developed during your time studying for a degree, yet many students do not take full advantage of the opportunities available to extend their capabilities. Study skills, the ways in which you understand course materials and convey your views to others, may be more relevant in this respect than the substantive content of your courses.

Problem-Solving

Tackling problems is a basic management activity in many walks of life. Typically the issues involved in career situations are very different from those involved in higher education. Problems are usually much more applied and immediate, needing to be tackled in a relatively short timescale, perhaps successively over several 'rounds' of the 'issue cycle'. In academic coursework referring to source materials can resolve many questions directly. But career problem-solving very rarely involves finding an answer in an external source. Career problems are much more individualized and diverse, requiring that you analyse a difficult situation directly, define a personal position, make the right commitment to one course of action, and live with the consequences. The familiar crutches of academic work are therefore unavailable, hence the importance which many employers ascribe to 'critical thinking' abilities in recruiting amongst graduates.

But unlike study tasks, career problems generally involve very similar sorts of issues recurring fairly frequently, so that over time you have more opportunity to become acquainted with the key questions. In most career contexts too, the range of options open for solving problems is fairly restricted by organizational directives, edicts from superiors, or the necessity of modifying existing practices only incrementally. One common style of managerial decision-making has been described by Lindblom (1959) as 'muddling through' – that is, deviating from the status quo only in small steps, and accomplishing changes piecemeal over successive reconsiderations of an issue. While academic problems in higher education tend to be presented as 'blank canvas' questions, with a wide range of allowable solutions, most career problem-solving takes place in a context already pre-structured by past decisions, inherited methods of working, and well-defined expectations.

The study skills which are likely to be most important for career problem-solving are the sort of 'brainstorming', idea-generating and lateral-thinking capabilities stressed in my discussion of concept clarification and essay writing. Academic questions are typically much more purely textual or conceptual than career problem-solving, where real outcomes turn immediately upon the choice of options. But lateral thinking and the ability to reconceptualize problems outside customary thought-paths are potentially important and valuable in almost all management contexts. Problem-solving in career contexts is usually not the product of individual cogitation but of interactive discussions between work colleagues.

Brainstorming and the generation of ideas tend to be more oral and less orientated to written materials than in higher education, reflecting the importance of decision-making in meetings or committees in most graduate career paths.

Working in Committees

Attending committee meetings is a central activity in any medium- or large-sized organization. Committees have become one of the most prevalent forms of organization both in public agencies and in private-sector corporations, partly as a corollary of increasing professionalization of their managerial and planning personnel (Galbraith, 1969). People bring to their careers an increased freight of educational and technical qualifications. Also, functional roles inside large modern organizations are much more specialized. So it is no longer possible for a simple hierarchical pattern of authority to produce sensible decisions in most areas of state or business activity. Instead, committees and meetings bring together a diversity of people, each narrowly informed in one specialism and also authoritative in that area of knowledge. Ideas and decisions then emerge out of the interaction between committee participants, with different policy considerations and areas of expertise focused down on to the particular problem in question.

Committee decision-making is invariably expensive, since it involves assembling several highly qualified personnel, often from scattered locations with substantial travel time lost in addition to the meeting time involved. Because they are costly occasions, and because oral discussions can be rather diffuse, most recurring meetings of this kind rapidly acquire a considerable formal structure – properly kept minutes, elaborate report-making procedures, and strongly developed conventions against going back on previous decisions. Hence their operation is cumulative, with policy decisions and areas of debate evolving over time. Coming on to a new committee always involves serving an 'apprenticeship period' (which may be quite lengthy) during which you stay relatively silent and acquire the background knowledge to be able to participate. In addition, because of the formal yet interactive quality of committees it is always important to appreciate the small-group dynamics operating between the personalities involved, and to find ways of putting points which people from different backgrounds and with different interests will find acceptable or compelling.

The importance of being able to persuade work colleagues to your point of view is rarely appreciated by students in higher education. Whether you are employed in business, the professions, or public-sector agencies, the whole character of your worklife may depend upon being able to actively sell your ideas in committee. Months of preparatory work, projects in which your section have got heavily involved or with which you are personally identified, mean that you go into these kinds of meetings with far more at stake than when you were a student. Yet while at college relatively few people make any deliberate effort to try to take fellow participants in classes or seminars along with their viewpoint. The purpose of participation in study discussions can be seen (both by those who join in and by those who stay silent) in terms of point-scoring or 'showing off' knowledge to the class teacher, rather than in terms of a co-operative effort to improve understanding.

This kind of approach is not surprising, given the individualized nature of most student activity in higher education. But the missed opportunities involved are considerable. Seminars, class discussions or group tutorials are a very important part of student life. They should provide you with invaluable opportunities first to observe and understand small-group dynamics, and second to develop essential personal skills in yourself through trying to influence or manage the flow of discussion. The fact that your fellow class participants are not self-selected (unlike friendship groups or student societies), and that classes have a formal structure which you cannot easily alter, makes them more similar to committees than most other groups in which students get involved. Knowing how to encourage shy participants, how to stimulate people who have switched off, how to smooth out frictions, how to make progress in discussion, how to secure acceptance of agreed points, and how to shut up obtrusive or overly voluble participants – all these are skills which can be important to you in a later career. Consequently, seminar management is not something which you should resignedly leave class teachers to grapple with. It is rather an opportunity to begin practising a key life skill.

Oral Presentation

Explaining issues is another essential part of committee work which can be developed in study discussions. Effective communication skills are explicitly included in some forms of assessment in higher education, at least to the extent that class teachers or tutors grade students on 'participation' in group debates. But in the humanities and social sciences there are relatively few class teachers who make a concerted effort to help students to give more effective oral presentations. Consequently students often approach 'giving a paper' to a class by mumbling their way through a complete essay, or alternatively talking very loosely around a set of disorganized notes. There are relatively few courses still where students have to pre-circulate a written paper and then give a separate and interesting oral presentation to their consequently more informed and more critical colleagues. Many people still go through their courses without ever drawing up an overhead projector slide or using any piece of equipment more complicated than blackboard chalk.

Oral presentations are much more important in subsequent career activities for a number of reasons. More of your work will take place in groups. Committees and meetings·are important milestones in the development of projects and ideas in all large organizations. Because they are expensive, meetings are usually fairly short, requiring you to express viewpoints precisely and briefly, to react effectively to comments and queries, and to stimulate and guide effective discussion arising from your presentation. Even if you do not have to put up a case to a whole meeting, you will frequently have to explain ideas orally in a brief compass to rushed superiors, when much the same capabilities will be needed. Equally, if your career involves managing a group of personnel ranked below you in an organizational hierarchy you may frequently have to introduce new procedures or analyse complex problems with colleagues, where a competent presentation will be expected. Finally, the technology of meeting and conference presentations has changed rapidly in the last few years, especially in marketing and related areas of private business, but also in many professional contexts. Overhead projector slides have increasingly been supplemented by computer slides and graphics, audio-visual slide shows, and video presentations.

Again higher education affords considerable opportunities to practise oral presentation skills. Some of the more expensive equipment of conference presentations – such as videobeam installations – are still far from commonplace in universities and polytechnics. But the more fundamental art of using subheadings and visual representations to clarify the themes and ideas in a talk can be carried a long way by using overhead projectors or large write-pads, which should be available in almost any classroom. And the essential personal skills involved in giving a clear, brief oral exposition to accompany a paper can be exercised routinely in any study group discussion.

Report Writing

Producing reports is also a central career activity. Business and professional reports are significantly different from essays in a number of respects. Reports are always written to a brief, usually laid down by superiors in an organizational hierarchy, or in a request from a meeting or a committee. The objectives of the report are thus fixed externally. The audience is often pressed for time – an attitude cultivated by higher-ranked decision-makers in all large organizations. People may also be deliberately critical; for example, in a committee those members with different interests from your organization or section may try to 'rubbish' your reports. Hence there is a premium on reports being as short as possible, clearly addressed to a manageable problem, and yet comprehensive in their coverage, including all the relevant available material. By contrast with the stress placed on 'style' and 'original thought' in academic work, effective reports are written in concise language, without flowery phrasing, with a minimum of rhetoric, and with a dominant factual or analytic drive. Reports clarify problems – in a way which can resemble the debugging of essay questions outlined in Chapter 4. They define options –

usually involving incremental departures from the status quo. And they suggest a decision. By contrast with the concern in much academic work to find a 'single best solution', most reports in business or the professions recommend courses of action which are 'robust' or risk-minimizing; which tackle problems in a satisfactory way, and which command agreement without necessarily being an optimal position.

Clearly written, well-organized essays, addressing specific questions, outlining alternative viewpoints and suggesting a conclusion can provide an invaluable training for report writing. Even the mechanics of producing essays, assembling and processing materials in a limited time-span, sketching a plan and composing a sequence of paragraphs, may correspond quite closely with later career activities. For example, one explanation for the continuing predominance of 'Oxbridge' arts graduates in recruitment to the British civil service argues that essays written up in three or four days after a swift scan through the libraries form a good preparation for drafting responses to parliamentary questions at short notice, working mainly from departmental files and previous minutes and decisions.

Only certain types of essay writing can help you produce better reports in a subsequent career. Long, self-indulgent and self-focused essays, crafted over for weeks, which extensively reproduce existing source materials or which do not develop a critical, personal viewpoint are unlikely to be a very helpful preparation. Similarly essays based only on theoretical proofs or empirical research certainties may inhibit your willingness to make informed judgements in the conditions of imperfect information which always characterize managerial and professional work. Effective report writing is most likely to be developed by frequent short essays produced to a definite timetable, directly and precisely tackling an externally set question, selecting relevant information from a mass of new data by means of a tightly organized relational argument – and emphasizing a critical assessment of different viewpoints or courses of action, the surfacing of assumptions, the clarification of values, and the development of judgemental abilities as guidelines in conditions of uncertainty.

Other Personal Skills

Some other skills are more routine but frequently used capabilities in a later career.

(a) **Keyboard literacy**, the ability to type or to use a wordprocessing system, is important in many occupations where extensive secretarial support is rare, such as journalism, writing, or higher education. However, the embodiment of secretarial skills in cheaper fixed capital commodities, such as multi-use work stations, and the trend towards electronic mail will both reinforce the trend for more professionals and managers to use keyboards directly.

(b) **Computer literacy** entails having a good intuitive grip on the logic of computer programs and of the main generic types of software package. Experience in simple micro-computing tasks – such as writing a few programmes in BASIC, and using wordprocessing, information retrieval, or quantitative analysis systems – can provide the foundations of computer literacy and allow you to adapt to the idiosyncrasies of the particular machines and software which you later work with. While you are studying at degree level you should take up any opportunities to work on your college's computers, especially if 'computer familiarization' short courses are provided outside the framework of formal instruction. The less you use computers in 'normal' coursework, the more important it could be to chase up these opportunities for acquiring 'hands on' experience.

(c) In many occupations **a good intuitive grasp on basic statistics** is useful. You need to know how to quickly simplify tables of figures; some easy rules of thumb which can help you to 'explore' data directly; how to get an idea of the level, range and 'shape' of a frequency distribution; and how to detect the underlying trend in a set of overtime statistics. The techniques of 'exploratory data analysis', developed in the USA by Tukey and others are more useful than 'classical' statistics, with their off-putting emphasis on mathematical formulae and significance tests. Many courses run by statistics departments are anachronistic for non-specialists because the mathematical operations which they emphasize are now as easy to perform on micro-computers as long-division on a pocket calculator. If you are a beginner in statistics you chiefly need a course explaining which techniques are appropriate for different problems; what basic operations are performed by a technique; how to interpret the output which computer programs produce; and the most common ways in which techniques can be abused or results misinterpreted. With interactive data analysis systems (such as SCSS) you can learn much of this on the computer itself by a process of trial and error.

(d) Similarly, it is worth trying to acquire **a basic understanding of how business accounts are constructed** and of how issues such as the financing of capital investment can be managed. For students not on accounting or management degrees many colleges now run 'business familiarization' courses which cover key aspects of this knowledge.

(e) **An understanding of information systems** should be one of the by-product skills which anybody acquires from three or four years of studying at degree level. Information systems of course include indexing systems, libraries, statistical sources, abstracting services, records offices, or computerized data bases. These forms of accessing information may seem very diverse, but they operate in fundamentally similar ways. The skills needed to extract full value from a big library – such as inventiveness in looking up keywords in a microfiche index, or a grasp on the different categories under which materials can be filed – are much the same as those used in consulting a computerized data base. Consequently putting in effort to diversify your materials and understand the information systems you use at college can have longer term benefits than simply producing a better essay for next week's class.

7.2 DIFFERENCES BETWEEN WORK ENVIRONMENTS AND THE STUDY ENVIRONMENT

Business firms, research and development organizations, public-sector agencies, and the 'social', business or 'technical' professions vary greatly in many respects: such as the size of organizations and work units; the importance of formal hierarchies; the nature of the work tasks involved; and the 'organizational culture' which grows up among their personnel. Some 'mechanistic' organizations have a highly rank-structured atmosphere. They place a premium on seniority and on compliance with pre-set rules or regulations in making decisions, and are often characterized by strongly emphasized 'departmentalism' and very formal co-ordination between sections. By contrast, more 'organismic' firms and agencies rely increasingly on fluid, project-based work groups, formed to tackle a particular problem. Here individuals have more work autonomy; seniority is less important relative to the possession of relevant expertise; and departmental loyalties are more constrained.

Despite these (and other) variations between organizations, there seem to be four respects in which studying at degree level can be a rather poor preparation for later career experiences.

(a) **Working in large organizations** is an aspect of career experiences about which students gain few insights while in higher education. This claim may seem surprising. After all, many higher education institutions can seem intimidatingly impersonal environments. Compared with schools or less advanced colleges, they are quite large, and have fewer fixed points of reference for individuals, such as class sets or peer groups. Students have to deal with a wide variety of more or less remote teachers. These relationships are usually hierarchical, and can be quite conflictual if you perform badly in coursework or find yourself radically out of sympathy with the subject approach adopted in your department.

Yet despite these characteristics, universities and polytechnics remain essentially distinct from most career organizations in a number of respects. First, colleges are basically 'humanist' and individually orientated rather than 'task-orientated' organizations. Their status is measured chiefly in terms of their ability to attract good students and motivate them to succeed. However confident or 'arrogant' academic institutions may look to students or to outsiders, they are very dependent on students' involvement. Of course, universities and polytechnics have well-developed incentives to encourage active participation, such as academic successes and better references. But they possess very few coercive powers over students, except in cases of the most conspicuous non-attendance.

In this sense, higher education institutions are basically voluntary organizations. How much work gets done depends very largely on individual students. Students have no formal working hours within which they have to account for their time to a direct superior. They are also the only people who suffer directly from failure to complete work, although teachers naturally wish to have as few 'failures' as possible on their books. Similarly students do most of their learning on their own. They do not usually have to work co-operatively with other students except friends, neither is their success dependent on other people completing intrinsically connected work tasks. It can be limiting if teachers do not comment promptly or usefully on written work, or if fellow students put little effort into classes. But these failings will not decisively affect anyone's success. Even in courses with the heaviest teaching or practical loads, each student is basically quite self-reliant.

By contrast, most work organizations are more coercive bodies, and most graduate career paths require very close interaction with colleagues and a high level of dependence upon the efforts of other people. Business corporations, government agencies or professional firms are much more hierarchical environments than a college or university. You are expected to clock-on at a regular time, to give a detailed account of how you allocate your working day between different tasks, to meet deadlines, take responsibilities, accept orders or meet expectations which are imposed by superiors, and generally behave in quite detailed ways (such as dress and mannerisms) in conformity with other people's values. Career organizations also have central goals which are quite separate from the development of their members' own lives and capabilities. However 'caring' or 'soulful' their personnel policies may be painted, their basic evaluation of you will depend on how much you contribute to the attainment of a corporate goal, not on an overall assessment of your qualities. Whether the corporate goal involves higher profits, maximum sales, the efficient implementation of public policy, or the smooth management of a social service, may be less important than the basic fact that you are valued not for yourself but for your instrumentality in meeting someone else's purposes.

This is not to say that large organizations are always (or even usually) alienating work environments. For many ambitious professionals and managers, career activities form a dominant part of their life-purposes and satisfactions. Especially in their twenties or thirties, people may be far more obsessed with their work than they ever were involved in academic study. But even among this group, their commitment often conflicts with dislike of the organization's rank hierarchy, and a recognition that their career ambitions depend heavily on overall organizational performance. And without this level of commitment, working in large organizations can be experienced as a soul-destroying pecuniary necessity. Many graduates feel that their work tasks are inherently boring and use only a fraction of their capabilities; and they find the necessity to take or give orders frustrating and personally demeaning.

A second fundamental difference about working in large organizations which I noted above is that the effectiveness of your own work depends heavily on other people's efforts and reactions. Few students straight from school have had much opportunity to develop abilities to get on with colleagues or to manage personal relations with superiors in an organizational hierarchy. In higher education, apart from contacts with the teaching staff, you will quite rarely have to work alongside or co-operate with people whom you have not chosen as colleagues. By contrast, in any substantial organization you will of necessity have extensive dealings with people who operate on a different wavelength, and have radically divergent values, views and priorities.

(b) **Academic knowledge and institutional know-how** are quite distinct. Academic values stress high-quality, professionalized or authoritative information. The methods of producing knowledge in the humanities and social sciences are highly formalized, time-consuming, and orientated to the long term. Durable information is highly prized by comparison with up-to-date but ephemeral data. Parsimonious theoretical formulations or abstractions which apply to a wide range of situations are accorded particular prestige. The procedures used to generate knowledge are vital to its status in academic work, so questions of method are as important as substantive truth value. The standard approach to problems is a frontal analytic attack, in which a herculean effort is made mentally to repicture all aspects of the problem and to produce a single comprehensive and optimal solution. The supreme value of academic work is always rationality, conceived in terms of a strict adherence to logical thought processes and a systematic method of inquiry. Books and papers in the humanities and social sciences are usually written up in a form which cultivates what Lindblom and Cohen (1979, p. 79) term an image of 'hyper-rationalism'. The role of guesswork, intuition, and chance in influencing the authors' analysis is systematically suppressed, even in those disciplines which rather deliberately eschew claims to follow a 'scientific' method.

By contrast, institutional know-how is the applied variant of common sense thinking. It is developed by people working in any large organization or specialized field of activity. Unlike academic knowledge, know-how is rarely codified or written down, chiefly because it is very situationally specific. Knowledge which is useful in one context is out of place in other situations. Institutional know-how is often a kind of folklore. People's direct experience of particular problems or organizations is extended and embroidered by oral story-telling, covering incidents or histories which have not been directly experienced. Hence know-how develops interactively, in conversation. It culminates in 'rules of thumb', rough and ready guidelines about what to do in different circumstances. Like most common sense, these generalizations usually cover situations where they are rather unlikely to be disputed or falsified. Consequently, the 'conventional wisdom' of organizations can seem minimalistic, retelling the obvious rather than helping to explore unfamiliar territory. Institutional know-how also emphasizes 'satisficing' solutions, which can be accepted by all the actors involved, rather than trying to achieve the optimal result demanded by academic criteria.

One of the most frequent criticisms made by established people of new graduates 'straight out of college' is their over-reliance on academic or theoretical knowledge and their lack of deference to institutional know-how. This line of comment can just be a stereotyping response, but it does reflect a general problem that graduates often lack insight into how decisions actually get made in their career field. 'Real life' problems and situations are characteristically much more 'messy' or unstructured than theoretical models, or even the carefully filleted case-studies analysed in the most applied social sciences (such as accounting, business studies, or social work). Time and cost constraints are more pressing; the opposition to unfamiliar methods of analysis is more 'political'; and the resistance to innovation is always more deep-rooted than someone new to an organization would expect. Hunches, guesswork, customary assumptions, latent values, a set of hidden or unspoken ways of seeing the world – all these inevitably influence the ways in which decisions are made.

It is difficult for people on degree courses fresh from school to develop institutional know-how about their eventual career path. Most students have fairly vague ideas about what they would (realistically) like to do, and no guarantees about where they will end up working. If you are on a sandwich course or have a scholarship from a firm where you put in work during the vacations, then you are privileged in this respect. Otherwise if you are keen to develop an awareness of how complex organizations work, the most useful aspects of your period in higher education may come from participation in activities such as student politics, running students' union activities, writing for the college newspaper, or simply trying to work out the 'internal politics' of your institution and its staff. These activities are valuable in reminding you that academic knowledge is in no sense a paradigm for all knowledge, certainly not for the kind of know-how which is most commonly deployed in career activities.

(c) **Managing commitments** in most career paths require that you develop fairly consistent patterns of individual working. In most professional and management jobs there is a continuous pressure of demands on time and of activities to fit inside pre-set deadlines. Correspondence accumulates daily and has to be answered within an acceptable period. Problems and queries have to be turned round regularly if your desk is not to become filled to overflowing. Some tasks are less pleasant than others, creating strong internal desires to postpone completing them. In a study environment these may slip altogether or get postponed indefinitely, with consequences only for yourself. But in a work environment superiors or subordinates, colleagues or clients, depend on your having taken appropriate action. It is for these reasons that all kinds of employers in their job descriptions tend to stress the importance of personal qualities such as 'application', reliability, precision, or conscientiousness. Working to deadlines is to some extent a knack which studying at universities and polytechnics does develop, especially if you acquire the ability to pace your own work output without detailed supervision. But only people with a very active 'second calling' as union politician, student journalist or amateur actress are likely to accumulate a portfolio of conflicting obligations which approximates that confronting ambitious graduates in most occupations.

(d) **A narrowing of your work interests** is implied in almost any transition from a study environment to managerial or professional work. In the humanities and social sciences you will at best reuse only a fraction of the material covered in three or four years' study. In most career paths academic knowledge only forms a background to much more applied decision-making. Even with a 'training' form of degree, only a few of the procedures or methods encountered in your studies are likely to be continuously relevant in your work. Partly this reflects the greater specialization of most work tasks compared with studying. Many graduates bemoan the loss of variety involved in transferring from degree study in at least four or five subjects a year to very standardized job demands. Academic work values individual inventiveness, originality, and the cultivation of a distinctive 'style' as an index of self-realization and self-development. Emphasis is placed on generating new ideas and knowledge, assembling adequate information to make a 'rational' decision, appreciating basic concepts and theories, and getting involved in fundamental controversies and debates. The humanistic values of higher education foster the feeling of being engaged in a process with a self-developmental rhythm. By contrast, even if your employers pursue enlightened personnel development policies and invest heavily in 'human capital' – for example, by rotating graduate trainees to diversify their work experiences – you are still likely to notice and deplore some major restrictions of your interests and activities compared with a study environment.

Summary of Suggestions: Turning Study Skills into Life Skills

1. Develop committee skills in classes and seminars by participating actively to try to achieve co-operative outcomes and to manage discussion (p. 170).

2. Use classes, seminars and tutorials as opportunities to develop skills in oral presentation. Be aware that oral skills are very important in many career paths (p. 171).

3. Develop report-writing skills by writing frequent, short essays, responding to externally set questions, outlining alternative views but reaching a reasoned conclusion, and set out clearly in an organized fashion (p. 173).

4. Take steps to become computer literate and statistically numerate at college. If possible, learn how to use a keyboard and understand basic accounts. Become adept at using information systems (p. 174).

5. Recognize the importance of institutional know-how and the interdependence of your work with that of others in all large work organizations. Use opportunities to develop this awareness while you are still at college (p. 180).

6. Use study deadlines and work tasks to develop your ability to manage commitments (p. 181).

7. Work out in advance the similarities and differences between study activities and your likely career tasks. Try to anticipate those personal skills which you may need in the future but which academic work only partly develops (p. 167).

Appendix 1. Resource Books for the Humanities and Social Sciences

This appendix lists sources of information for twelve disciplines in the humanities and fifteen in the social sciences. In each subject up to five kinds of resource book may be included:

'Think books' – discuss the rationale, central focus or philosophy' of the discipline; or they may outline current controversies within it; or they may explain how to go about studying it;

Histories – describe the modern development of the subject and the evolution of professional debates;

Dictionaries – are specialist subject dictionaries, which define and explain key concepts, terms and theories;

Reference – are major reference sources specific to the discipline;

Journals for reviews – are journals with more extensive book review sections.

Where there are multiple 'think books' and histories I have listed the more basic books first and the more complex accounts later on.

My criterion for resource books is that they should aid students fairly early on in a degree course to appraise and understand their subjects more self-consciously. I have also deliberately avoided mentioning textbooks, collections of essays, and books whose large scale is off-putting. Hence most of the 'think books' and histories offer short or medium-length guides to the evolution of and current debate in the discipline. Lastly, the vast bulk of the 'think books', histories and dictionaries are currently in print and available in paperback. By contrast, the reference books cited are usually accessible only in libraries.

You should follow the suggestions in Chapter 2 and skim through any 'think book', history or dictionary before purchasing it or investing time in trying to read it. 'Think books' especially are very diverse and written from many different angles, so check that the book looks relevant to your specific interests and is written in a style which appeals to you. The need to pick and choose is greatest where the listings include a great many choices. In other subjects the problem may be that 'think books' or even histories of the disciplines are rarely written. Finally, my research and consultation with colleagues in compiling these listings may well have gaps. Hence, some useful sources might have been missed off due to my limited knowledge rather than because of a judgement that they were not worth including. Consequently additions to and comments on the listings would be gratefully received.

For the Social Sciences turn to page 192

1 HUMANITIES SUBJECTS

Archaeology	Foreign literature
Architecture	History
Arts	Linguistics
Classical studies	Literature studies
Drama	Philosophy
English	Religious studies

Archaeology

Think books: P. Rahtz, *Invitation to Archaeology* (Oxford: Blackwell, 1985); D. L. Clarke, *Analytical Archaeology* (London: Methuen, 1978).

Histories: G. Daniel, *150 Years of Archaeology* (London: Duckworth, 1975).

Dictionaries: R. D. Whitehouse, *Macmillan Dictionary of Archaeology* (London: Macmillan, 1983); W. Bray and D. Trump, *Penguin Dictionary of Archaeology* (Harmondsworth: Penguin, 1982).

Architecture

Histories: C. Jencks, *Modern Movements in Architecture* (Harmondsworth: Penguin, 1977).
Dictionaries: J. Fleming, H. Honour and N. Pevsner, *The Penguin Dictionary of Architecture* (Harmondsworth: Penguin, 1980); G. Hatje (ed.), *Encylopaedia of Modern Architecture* (London: Thames and Hudson, 1963).
Journals for   *Architectural Review*; *Journal of the Royal Institute of*
reviews: *British Architects.*

Arts

Think books: H. Read, *The Philosophy of Modern Art* (London: Faber, 1964); H. B. Chipp, *Theories of Modern Art* (Berkeley: University of California Press, 1968); B. Tilghman, *But Is It Art?* (Oxford: Blackwell, 1984); J. Hospers (ed.), *Introductory Readings in Aesthetics* (New York: Free Press, 1969); R. Scruton, *Art and Imagination* (London: Routledge and Kegan Paul, 1982).
Histories: M. Dufrenne, *Main Trends in Aesthetics and the Sciences of Art* (New York; Homes and Meier, 1978); F. Frascina and C. Harrison, *Modern Art and Modernism: A Critical Anthology* (London: Harper and Row, 1986).

Dictionaries: P. and L. Murray, *The Penguin Dictionary of Art and Artists* (Harmondsworth: Penguin, 1983); K. McLeish, *The Penguin Companion to Arts in the Twentieth Century* (Harmondsworth; Penguin, 1985); H. Osborne (ed.), *The Oxford Companion to Twentieth-Century Art* (London: Oxford University Press, 1981).

Reference: H. Osborne (ed.), *The Oxford Companion to Art* (London: Oxford University Press, 1979); H. Osborne (ed.), *The Oxford Companion to the Decorative Arts* (Oxford: Oxford University Press, 1985); J. Fleming and H. Honour, *The Penguin Dictionary of Decorative Arts* (London: Allen Lane, 1977).

Journals for reviews: *Notes and Queries*; *Art History*.

Classical Studies

Dictionaries: R. A. Talbert *et al.*, *Atlas of Classical History* (London: Croom Helm, 1985).

Reference: N. G. Hammond and H. H. Scullard. *The Oxford Classical Dictionary* (Oxford: Clarendon Press, 1970); C. B. Avery, *The New Century Classical Handbook* (London: Harrop, 1962).

Journals for reviews: *Classical Review*.

Drama
(See also – English, Literature Studies)

Think books: C. R. Reaske, *How to Analyse Drama* (New York: Monarch Press, 1984); R. Hayman, *How to Read* a *Play* (London: Eyre Methuen: 1979); M. Esslin, *An Anatomy of Drama* (London: Sphere, 1978).

Reference: P. Hartnoll, *The Concise Oxford Companion to the Theatre* (London: Oxford University Press, 1972).

English
(See also – Literature Studies)

Think books: M. Boulton, *The Anatomy of Literary Studies: An Introduction to the Study of English Literature* London: Routledge and Kegan Paul, 1980); R. L. Brett, *An Introduction to English Studies* (London: Arnold, 1976); A. T. Ross (ed.), *English: An Outline for the Intending Student* (London: Routledge and Kegan Paul, 1971); C. S. Lewis, *An Experiment in Criticism* (Cambridge: Cambridge University Press, 1961); F. R. Leavis, *English Literature in Our Time and the Universities* (London: Chatto and Windus, 1969).

Histories: B. Ford (ed.), *A Guide for Readers of the Pelican Guide to English Literature* (Harmondsworth: Penguin, 1984).

Reference: M. Drabble (ed.), *The Oxford Companion to English Literature* (Oxford: Oxford University Press, 1985).

Journals for reviews: *The Times Literary Supplement*; *The New York Review of Books*; *The Review of English Studies*; *English Studies*; *American Studies*; *Eighteenth Century Studies*.

Foreign Literature
(See also – Literature Studies)

Think books: T. Todorov, *French Literary Theory Today* (Cambridge: Cambridge University Press, 1982).

Dictionaries: J. M. Reid, *The Concise Oxford Dictionary of French Literature* (Oxford: Oxford University Press, 1976); P. Wood, *The Oxford Companion to Spanish Literature* (Oxford: Oxford University Press, 1978); J. Paxton, *A Companion to Russian History* (London: Batsford, 1983).

Journals for reviews: *Modern Languages Review*; *French Studies*.

History

Think books: E. H. Carr, *What Is History?* (Harmondsworth: Penguin, 1969); G. H. Elton, *The Practice of History* (London: Fontana, 1967); H. Butterfield, *The Whig Interpretation of History* (Harmondsworth: Penguin: 1973; J. Tosh. *The Pursuit of History* (London: Longman, 1984) P. Dray, *Perspectives on History* (London: Routledge and Kegan Paul, 1980); D. Beddoe, *Discovering Women's History: A Practical Manual* (London: Routledge and Kegan Paul, 1983); D. Lowenthal, *The Past is a Foreign Country* (Cambridge: Cambridge University Press, 1985); A. Marwick, *The Nature of History* (London: Macmillan, 1981); B. Tuchmann, *Practising History* (London: Macmillan, 1983); J. Kelly, *Women, History and Theory* (Chicago: University of Chicago Press, 1984); P. Wright, *On Living in an Old Country* (London: New Left Books, 1985); R. G. Collingwood, *The Idea of History* (Oxford: Clarendon Press, 1961).

Histories: J. Kenyon, *The History Men: The Historical Profession in England since the Renaissance* (London: Weidenfeld and Nicolson, 1983); G. Barraclough, *Main Trends in History* (New York: Holmes and Meier, 1978); H. J. Kaye, *The British Marxist Historians* (Oxford: Polity Press, 1984).

Dictionaries: C. Cook, *Dictionary of Historical Terms* (London: Macmillan, 1981); A. Palmer, *The Penguin Dictionary of Twentieth-Century History 1900–82* (Harmondsworth: Penguin, 1983); A. Palmer, *The Penguin Dictionary of Modern History, 1789–1945* (Harmondsworth: Penguin, 1977): E. N. Williams, *Penguin Dictionary of English and European History, 1485–1789* (Harmondsworth: Penguin, 1980): A. and V. Palmer, *A Dictionary of Historical Quotations* (London: Paladin, 1985).

Journals for reviews: *English Historical Review*; *History*; *The American Historical Review*; *Journal of American History*; *Reviews in American History*; *Journal of Modern History*; *Journal of Interdisciplinary History*; *Social History*; *Journal of Social History*; *European History Quarterly*.

Linguistics

Think books: D. Crystal, *What Is Linguistics?* (London: Arnold, 1985); K. Brown, *Linguistics Today* (London; Fontana, 1984); D. Crystal, *Linguistics* (Harmondsworth: Penguin, 1971).

Histories: G. Sampson, *Schools of Linguistics* (London: Hutchinson, 1980).

Dictionaries: D. Crystal, *A Dictionary of Linguistics and Phonetics* (Oxford: Blackwell, 1985): O. Ducrot and T. Todorov, *Encyclopaedic Dictionary of the Sciences of Language* (Oxford: Blackwell, 1981).

Journals for reviews: *Journal of Linguistics*; *Language*.

Literature Studies
(See also – English, Foreign Literature)

Think books: J. Peck, *How to Study a Novel* (London: Macmillan, 1983); J. Hawthorn, *Studying the Novel* (London: Arnold, 1985); D. Daiches, *Critical Approaches to Literature* (London: Longman, 1982); T. Eagleton, *Literary Theory: An Introduction* (Oxford: Blackwell, 1983); G. H. Hartmann, *Criticism in the Wilderness* (New Haven: Yale University Press, 1983); W. Gerrin, E. Labor, L. Morgan and J. R. Willingham, *A Handbook of Critical Approaches to Literature* (New York: Harper and Row, 1979); J. Gribble, *Literary Education: A Re-evaluation* (Cambridge: Cambridge University Press, 1983); I. A. Richards, *Principles of Literary Criticism* (London: Routledge and Kegan Paul, 1983); F. W. Bateson, *The Scholar-Critic* (London, Routledge and Kegan Paul: 1972); S. Fish, *Is There a Text in This Class?* (Cambridge, Mass.: Harvard University Press, 1980); G. Graff, *Literature Against Itself: Literary Ideas in Modern Society* (Chicago: University of Chicago Press, 1979); J. P. Sartre, *What is Literature?* (London: Methuen, 1967).

Histories: E. Borklund, *Contemporary Literary Critics* (London: Macmillan, 1982).

Dictionaries: R. Fowler, *A Dictionary of Modern Critical Terms* (London: Routledge and Kegan Paul, 1973); J. A. Cudden, *A Dictionary of Literary Terms* (Harmondsworth: Penguin, 1985); M. H. Abrams, *A Glossary of Literary Terms* (New York: Holt, Rinehart and Winston, 1981).

Philosophy

Think books: M. Hollis, *Invitation to Philosophy* (Oxford: Oxford University Press, 1984); A. O'Hear, *What Philosophy Is* (Harmondsworth: Penguin, 1985); A. J. Ayer, *The Central Questions of Philosophy* (Harmondsworth: Penguin, 1973).

Histories: J. Passmore, *A Hundred Years of Philosophy* (Harmondsworth: Penguin, 1968); R. Scruton, *A Short History of Modern Philosophy* (London: Routledge and Kegan Paul, 1984); P. Ricoeur, *Main Trends in Philosophy* (New York: Holmes and Meier, 1978).

Dictionaries: A. Flew (ed.), *A Dictionary of Philosophy* (London: Pan, 1979).

Reference: P. Edwards (ed.), *The Encyclopaedia of Philosophy* (New York: Macmillan and Free Press, 1967), seven volumes.

Journals for reviews: *The Philosophical Review*; *Ethics*; *Journal of the History of Philosophy*.

Religious Studies

Think books: J. Holm, *The Study of Religions* (London: Sheldon Press, 1977); K. Nielson, *An Introduction to the Philosophy of Religion* (London: Macmillan, 1982).

Dictionaries: R.C. Zaehner, *The Concise Encyclopaedia of Living Faiths* (London: Hutchinson, 1977).

Reference: A. Richardson (ed.), *A Dictionary of Christian Theology* (London: SCM Press, 1969); J. Macquarrie (ed.), *A Dictionary of Christian Ethics* (London: SCM Press, 1967); G. Parrinder, *A Dictionary of Non-Christian Religions* (Amersham, Bucks: Hulton Educational Publications, 1971).

2 SOCIAL SCIENCES

Accounting	International relations
Anthropology	Law
Business studies	Politics/government
Economics	Psychology
Economic history	Social sciences in general
Education	Social administration
Geography	Sociology
Industrial relations	Urban studies

Accounting
(See also – Business Studies)

Dictionaries: A. H. Parker, *Macmillan Dictionary of Accounting* (London: Macmillan, 1984).

Anthropology

Think books: M. Auge, *The Anthropological Circle* (Cambridge: Cambridge University Press, 1982).

Histories: A. Kuper, *Anthropology and Anthropologists: The Modern British School* (London: Routledge and Kegan Paul, 1983); M. Freedman, *Main Trends in Social and Cultural Anthropology* (New York: Holmes and Meier, 1977); M. Bloch, *Marxism and Anthropology* (Oxford: Oxford University Press, 1983).

Dictionaries: C. Winick, *Dictionary of Anthropology* (Totowa, New Jersey: Rowman and Alanheld, 1977).

Journals for reviews: *American Anthropologist.*

Business Studies
(See also – Accounting, Industrial Relations)

Think books: P. Lawrence, *Invitation to Management* (Oxford: Blackwell, 1986).

Dictionaries: M. Greener, *The Penguin Dictionary of Commerce* (Harmondsworth: Penguin, 1970); J. L. Hansen, *A Dictionary of Economics and Commerce* (Plymouth: Macdonald and Evans, 1977); S. E. Stiegler, *A Dictionary of Economics and Business* (London: Pan, 1986); M. J. Baker, *Macmillan Dictionary of Marketing and Advertising* (London: Macmillan, 1974).

Reference: *The Good Book Guide for Business* (Harmondsworth: Penguin, 1984).

Economics

Think books: D. Whynes, *Invitation to Economics* (Oxford: Blackwell, 1985); S. E. Rhoads, *The Economist's View of the World* (Cambridge: Cambridge University Press, 1985); L. C. Thurow, *Dangerous Currents: The State of Economics* (Oxford: Oxford University Press, 1983).

Histories: J. K. Galbraith, *The Age of Uncertainty* (London: Deutsch, 1977); W. Barber, *A History of Economic Thought* (Harmondsworth: Penguin, 1967); A. K. Dasgupta, *Epochs of Economic Theory* (Oxford: Blackwell, 1985); P. Deane, *The Evolution of Economic Ideas* (Cambridge: Cambridge University Press, 1978); S. Dow, *Macroeconomic Thought*) (Oxford: Blackwell, 1985).

Dictionaries: D. W. Pearce, *The Macmillan Dictionary of Modern Economics* (London: Macmillan, 1983); G. Bannock, R. E. Baker and R. Rees, *The Penguin Dictionary of Economics* (Harmondsworth: Penguin, 1984); A. Seldon and F. G. Pennance,

Everyman's Dictionary of Economics (London: Dent, 1974); A. Gilpin, *A Dictionary of Economic Terms* (London: Butterworths, 1977).

Reference: M. Blaug and P. Sturges, *Who's Who in Economics* (Brighton: Wheatsheaf, 1983).

Journals for   *The Economic Journal*; *Economica.*
reviews:

Economic History

Think books: J. R. Hicks, *A Theory of Economic History* (London: Oxford University Press, 1969); D.C. North, *Structure and Change in Economic History* (New York: Norton, 1981).

Journals for   *Economic History Review.*
reviews:

Education

Think books: P. Hirst, *Educational Theory and its Foundation Disciplines* (London: Routledge and Kegan Paul, 1983); T. W. Moore, *Educational Theory: An Introduction* (London: Routledge and Kegan Paul, 1974); P. Hirst and R. S. Peters, *The Logic of Education* (London: Routledge and Kegan Paul, 1970); K. Thompson, *Education and Philosophy* (Oxford: Blackwell, 1974).

Histories: G. F. Kneller, *Movements of Thought in Modern Education* (New York: Wiley, 1984).

Dictionaries: D. Rowntree, *A Dictionary of Education* (London: Harper and Row, 1981); P. Gordon and D. Lawton, *A Guide to English Educational Terms*, (London: Batsford, 1984); P. J. Hills, *A Dictionary of Education* (London: Routledge and Kegan Paul, 1982); G. T. Page and J. B.

Thomas, *International Dictionary of Education* (London: Kogan Page, 1977).

Reference: T. Husen and T. N. Postlewaite (eds), *International Encyclopaedia of Education* (Oxford: Pergamon, 1985), eight volumes.

Journals for   *British Journal of Educational Studies*; *Educational*
reviews: *Review*.

Geography
(See also – Urban Studies)

Think books: R. J. Johnston (ed.), *The Future of Geography* (London: Methuen, 1985); R. J. Johnston, *Geography and Geographers: Anglo-American Human Geography since 1945* (London: Arnold, 1983); D. Stoddart, *On Geography* (Oxford: Blackwell, 1986); R. J. Johnston, *Philosophy and Human Geography* (London: Arnold, 1983).

Histories: A. Holt-Jensen, *Geography: Its History and Concepts* (London: Harper and Row, 1980).

Dictionaries: J. Whittow, *The Penguin Dictionary of Physical Geography* (Harmondsworth: Penguin, 1984); M. Allaby, *Dictionary of the Environment* (London: Macmillan, 1977).

Journals for   *Geography*; *The Geographical Journal*; *Progress In*
reviews: *Physical Geography*; *Progress in Human Geography*; *The Professional Geographer*; *Journal of Historical Geography*.

Industrial Relations

Think books: T. Keenoy, *Invitation to Industrial Relations* (Oxford: Blackwell, 1985).

Journals for   *British Journal of Industrial Relations.*
reviews:

International Relations
(See also – Politics)

Think books: T. Taylor, *Approaches and Theory in International Relations* (London: Longman, 1978); J. Frankel, *Contemporary International Theory and the Behaviour of States* (London: Oxford University Press, 1973); J. C. Garnett, *Commensense and the Theory of International Politics* (London: Macmillan, 1984).

Histories: A. J. Groom and C. R. Mitchell, *International Relations Theory: A Bibliography* (London: Pinter, 1978).

Dictionaries: J. C. Plano and R. Olton, *The International Relations Dictionary* (Santa Barbara, California: ABC-Clio, 1980).

Journals for   *International History Review.*
reviews:

Law

Think books: P. Kenny, *Studying the Law* (London: Butterworths, 1985); G. Williams, *Learning the Law* (London: Stevens, 1982); H. L. A. Hart, *The Concept of Law* (Oxford: Clarendon Press, 1962); J. Harris, *Legal Philosophies* (London, Butterworths, 1980).

Histories: D. Lloyd, *The Idea of Law* (Harmondsworth: Penguin, 1985).

Dictionaries: L. B. Curzon, *A Dictionary of Law* (Plymouth: Macdonald and Evans, 1983); J. B. Saunders (ed.), *Mozley and Whiteley's Law Dictionary* (London: Butterworths, 1977).

Reference: J. Dane and P. A. Thomas, *How to Use a Law Library* (London: Sweet and Maxwell, 1979).
Journals for *Cambridge Law Journal*; *Public Law*.
reviews:

Politics/Government
(See also – International Relations

Think books: M. Laver, *Invitation to Politics* (Oxford: Martin Robertson, 1983); A. Leftwich (ed.), *What is Politics?* (Oxford: Blackwell, 1984); B. Crick, *In Defence of Politics* (Harmondsworth: Penguin, 1964); R. Miliband, *Marxism and Politics* (Oxford: Oxford University Press, 1977); J. Blondel, *The Discipline of Politics* (London: Butterworths, 1981).

Histories: W. J. McKenzie, *Politics and the Social Sciences* (Harmondsworth: Penguin, 1967).

Dictionaries: R. Scruton, *A Dictionary of Political Thought* (London: Pan 1982); D. Robertson, *The Penguin Dictionary of Politics* (Harmondsworth: Penguin, 1986); G. K. Roberts, *A Dictionary of Political Analysis* (London: Longman, 1971); D. Miller, J. Coleman, W. Connolly and A. Ryan (eds), *An Encyclopaedic Dictionary of Political Thought* (Oxford: Blackwell, 1986); V. Bogdanor (ed.), *A Dictionary of Political Institutions* (Oxford; Blackwell, 1987).

Journals for *Political Studies*; *American Political Science Review*;
reviews: *Journal of Politics*; *Public Administration*; *West European Politics*.

Psychology

Think books: D. Cohen, *Psychologists on Psychology* (London: Ark, 1985); A. Gale, *What is Psychology?* (London: Arnold, 1985); E. R. Valentine, *Conceptual Issues in Psychology* (London: Allen and Unwin, 1982).

Histories: R. Lowry, *The Evolution of Psychological Theory* (New York: Aldine, 1982).

Dictionaries: A. S. Reber, *The Penguin Dictionary of Psychology* (Harmondsworth: Penguin, 1985); L. Kristal (ed.), *The ABC of Psychology* (Harmondsworth: Penguin, 1982); F. Bruno, *A Dictionary of Key Words in Psychology* (London: Routledge and Kegan Paul, 1986).

Journals for reviews: *British Journal of Psychology*.

Social Administration
(See also – Sociology)

Think books: SOCIAL WORK

B. Jordan, *Invitation to Social Work* (Oxford: Blackwell, 1984); N. and R. Timms, *Perspectives in Social Work* (London: Routledge and Kegan Paul, 1977); H. England, *Social Work as Art: Making Sense for Good Practice* (London: Allen and Unwin, 1986); Z. T. Butrym, *The Nature of Social Work* (London: Macmillan, 1976).

SOCIAL POLICY

A. Forder, *Concepts in Social Administration* (London: Routledge and Kegan Paul, 1974); P. Taylor-Gooby and J. Dale, *Social Theory and Social Welfare* (London: Arnold, 1981); V. George and P. Wilding, *Ideology and Social Welfare* (London: Routledge and Kegan Paul, 1985); R. Mishra,

Society and Social Policy (London: Macmillan, 1977).

Journals for   *Journal of Social Policy*; *British Journal of Social*
reviews: *Work*.

Social Sciences in General

Think books: R. Trigg, *Understanding Social Science* (Oxford: Blackwell, 1985); C. Lindblom and D. Cohen, *Useable Knowledge: Social Science and Social Problem Solving* (New Haven: Yale University Press, 1979).

Dictionaries: H. Reading, *A Dictionary of the Social Sciences* (London: Routledge and Kegan Paul, 1977); A. Kuper and J. Kuper (eds), *The Social Science Encyclopaedia* (London: Routledge and Kegan Paul, 1985); P. McC. Miller and M. Wilson, *A Dictionary of Social Science Methods* (London: Wiley, 1983).

Reference: D. L. Sils (ed.), *International Encyclopaedia of the Social Sciences* (New York: Macmillan and Free Press, 1968), seventeen volumes.

Sociology

Think books: C. Wright Mills, *The Sociological Imagination* (Harmondsworth: Penguin, 1970); N. Elias, *What is Sociology?* (London: Hutchinson, 1978): A. Giddens, *New Rules of Sociological Method* (London: Hutchinson, 1979); P. Berger and H. Kellner, *Sociology Reinterpreted: An Essay on Method and Vocation* (Harmondsworth: Penguin, 1982).

Histories: H. Maus, *A Short History of Sociology* (London: Routledge and Kegan Paul, 1971); T. Bottomore and R. Nisbet (eds), *A History of Sociological Analysis* (London: Heinemann, 1978).

Dictionaries: M. Mann, *The Student's Companion to Sociology* (London: Macmillan, 1981); Duncan Mitchell, *A New Dictionary of Sociology* (London: Routledge and Kegan Paul, 1979); N. Abercrombie, S. Hill and B. S. Turner, *The Penguin Dictionary of Sociology* (Harmondsworth: Penguin, 1984); R. Boudon and F. Bourricaud, *A Critical Dictionary of Sociology* (London: Tavistock, 1987).

Journals for reviews: *Sociology*; *British Journal of Sociology*; *American Journal of Sociology*; *Social Forces*.

Urban Studies
(See also – Geography)

Think books: P. Saunders, *Social Theory and the Urban Question* (London: Heinemann, 1981): H. Stretton, *Urban Planning in Rich and Poor Countries* (Oxford: Opus, 1978).

Histories: P. Dunleavy, *The Scope of Urban Studies in Social Science* (Milton Keynes: Open University Press, 1982), Units 3–4, Open University Course D202: 'Urban Change and Conflict'.

Journals for reviews: *Urban Studies*; *International Journal of Urban and Regional Research*; *Journal of the American Planning Association*; *Town Planning Review*.

Appendix 2. Study Skills: Suggestions for Further Reading

All the books and articles cited here are still in print or generally available, for example in larger public libraries.

CHAPTER 1: STARTING OFF IN HIGHER EDUCATION

● There are a large number of books which deal with basic study skills, and make suggestions about the mechanics of getting down to work in a higher education context − for example, how to allocate your time, how to focus on your studies, and so on. They are intended for lower-level courses, but you should find them helpful if:

(i) you are particularly worried about how to be an effective student:

(ii) you feel quite lost about how best to tackle academic work, perhaps because you have been out of education for a long time; or

(iii) you are studying either part-time or on a correspondence course, with little or no direct contact with teachers.

Ashman, S. and George, A. (1980). *Study And Learn* (London: Heinemann).

Ellis, P. and Hopkins, K. (1985). *How to Succeed in Written Work and Study: A Handbook for Students* (London: Collins).

Fisher Cassie, W. and Constantine, T. (1977). *A Student's Guide to Success* (London: Macmillan).

Freeman, R. (1982). *Mastering Study Skills* (London: Macmillan).

Harman, C. and Freeman, R. (1984). *How to Study Effectively* (Cambridge: National Extension College), Correspondence Text ED07.

Marshall, L. A. and Rowland, F. (1983). *A Guide to Learning Independently* (Milton Keynes: Open University Press).

Palmer, R. and Pope, C. (1984). *Brain Train: Studying for Success* (London: Spon).

Rowntree, D. (1980). *Learn How to Study* (London: Macdonald).

Walter, T. and Siebert, A. (1984). *Student Success* (New York: Holt, Rinehart and Winston).

● Some books written mainly for lectures and teachers are useful for anyone involved in advising students or designing courses. Student readers might find them helpful also in appraising their teachers or evaluating the kinds of study counselling available in their college:

Beard, R. (1970), *Teaching and Learning in Higher Education* (Harmondsworth: Penguin).

Bligh, D.A. (1970). *What's the Use of Lectures?* (London: University Teaching Methods Unit).

Brown, G. (1978), *Lecturing and Explaining* (London: Methuen).

Entwhistle, N. (1977). 'Strategies of learning and studying: recent research findings', *British Journal of Educational Studies*, vol. 25.

Gibbs, G. (1981). *Teaching Students How to Learn* (Milton Keynes: Open University Press).

Hills, P. J. (ed.) (1979). *Study Courses and Counselling* (London: Society for Research into Higher Education).

Main, A. (1980). *Encouraging Effective Learning: An Approach to Study Counselling* (Edinburgh: Scottish Academic Press).

University Teaching Methods Unit (1978). *Improving Teaching in Higher Education* (London: 1978).

CHAPTER 2: GENERATING INFORMATION

● If you feel that you have a particular problem because you read slowly, the following books may be helpful. But be sceptical of claims that 'speed reading' techniques can somehow solve most problems in generating information. Efficient search and selection procedures are more important than your capacity to assimilate verbiage:

Buzan, T. (1977), *Speed Reading* (Newton Abbot: David and Charles).

de Leeuw, M. and E. (1964). *Read Better, Read Faster* (Harmondsworth: Penguin).

Dudley, G.A. (1986). *Double Your Learning Power: Master the Techniques of Successful Memory and Recall* (Wellingborough, Northants: Thorsons).

Webster, O. (1965). *Read Well and Remember* (London: Pan).

• One book with useful (non-obvious) suggestions on improving your skills in mastering information systems is:

Bell, D. C. (1984). *Tools in the Learning Trade: A Guide to Eight Indispensable Tools for College Students* (Metichen, New Jersey: Scarecrow Press).

• On note-taking:

Buzan, T. (1974). *Use Your Head* (London: BBC).

Elliot, K. and Wright, D. (no date). *Studying the Professional Way* (Worcester: Northwich).

CHAPTER 3: ANALYSING CONCEPTS AND THEORIES

• Dictionaries of synonyms which also supply antonyms and contrasting or analogous words may be useful in understanding individual concepts using the techniques described here. Two helpful sources are:

Cassells Modern Guide to Synonyms and Related Words (1979). (London: Cassells).

Webster's New Dictionary of Synonyms (1978). (Springfield, Mass.: Merriam).

• Some people find 'popular psychology' titles are worthwhile in stimulating them to re-examine the ways in which they handle concepts and problems:

Buzan, T. (1974). *Use Your Head* (London: BBC).
de Bono, E. (1970). *The Uses of Lateral Thinking* (Harmondsworth: Penguin).
de Bono, E. (1971). *The Mechanism of Mind* (Harmondsworth: Penguin).
Mace, C. (1969). *The Psychology of Study* (Harmondsworth: Penguin).

CHAPTER 4: WRITING ESSAYS

• Basic guides to improving essays are provided by:

Lewis, R. (1979). *How to Write Essays* (London: Macmillan).
Turk, C. (1979). *Effective Writing* (London: Spon).

• Books orientated more to creative writing, literary essays and advertising include:

Fairfax, J. and Moat, J. (1981). *The Way to Write* (London: Elm Tree/Hamish Hamilton).
Howard, G. (1980). *Getting Through! How to Make Words Work for You* (Newton Abbott: David and Charles).
Pirie, D. P. (1985). *How to Write Critical Essays* (London: Methuen).

• For extremely technical materials see:

Cooper, B. M. (1985). *Writing Technical Reports* (Harmondsworth: Penguin).
O'Connor, M. and Woodford, E. P. (1978). *Writing Scientific Papers in English* (Tunbridge Wells, Kent: Pitman Medical).

• On style issues, there are some genuinely useful manuals:

Baker, S. (1985). *The Practical Stylist* (New York: Harper and Row).
Gowers, E. (1978). *The Complete Plain Words* (Harmondsworth: Penguin).

Miller, C. and Swift, K. (1980). *The Handbook on Non-sexist Writing* (London: The Women's Press).
Weiner, E. S. and Hardin, J. M. (1984). *The Oxford Guide to the English Language* (Oxford, Oxford University Press).

CHAPTER 5: WRITING DISSERTATIONS

● Stimulating ideas on the interconnection between research and writing are included in:

Mills, C. W. (1973). 'On intellectual craftsmanship', in his book *The Sociological Imagination* (Harmondsworth: Penguin).
Elton, G. W. (1967). *The Practice of History* (London: Fontana).

● The following titles are useful in several ways:

Kane, E. (1984). *Doing Your Research: How to Do Basic Descriptive Research in the Social Sciences and Humanities* (London: Marion Boyars).
Madsen, D. (1983). *Successful Dissertations and Theses* (San Francisco: Josey Bass).

● Texts focusing only on the mechanics of writing and referencing dissertations include:

Berry, D. M. and Martin, G. P. (1971). *A Guide to Writing Research Papers* (New York: McGraw-Hill).
Campbell, W. G., Ballou, S. V. and Slade, C. (1982). *Form and Style: Theses, Reports, Term Papers* (Boston: Houghton Mifflin).
Turabian, K. L. (1963). *Students' Guide for Writing College Papers* (Chicago: University of Chicago Press).
Watson, G. (1970), *The Literary Thesis* (Harlow: Longman).

● Two valuable books about graduate work involving longer research theses are:

Sternberg, D. (1981). *How to Complete and Survive a Doctoral Dissertation* (New York: St. Martin's Press).

Stoch, M. (1985). *A Practical Guide to Graduate Research* (New York: McGraw-Hill).

CHAPTER 6: REVISING FOR EXAMS

The basic study skills books referenced for Chapter 1 above discuss how to devise a revision timetable and give commonsense advice.

CHAPTER 7: TURNING STUDY SKILLS INTO LIFE SKILLS

● The relationship between formal or academic knowledge and practical decision-making is usefully discussed in:

Lindblom, C. E. and Cohen, D. K. (1979). *Useable Knowledge: Social Science and Social Problem Solving* (New Haven: Yale University Press).

● On the internal operations of large organizations see:

Downs, A. (1967). *Inside Bureaucracy* (Boston: Little Brown).
Galbraith, J. K. (1969). *The New Industrial State* (Harmondsworth: Penguin).

● A valuable book for less confident women (and maybe men) is:
Bulter, R. (1981). *Self-Assertion for Women* (San Francisco: Harper and Row).

● Helpful hints on getting organized, and some insights into work pressures are provided by:

Turla, P. and Hawkins, L. (1985). *Time Management Made Easy* (London: Panther).

Bibliography

Ashman, S. and George, A. (1982). *Study and Learn* (London: Heinemann).

Bertalanffy, L. von (1973). *General System Theory* (Harmondsworth: Penguin).

Blau, P. M. and Nisbet, R. K. (1981). *Continuities in Structural Inquiry* (London: Sage).

Bligh, D.A. (1970). *What's the Use of Lectures?* (London: University Teaching Methods Unit).

Bullock, A. and Stalleybrass, O. (eds) (1983). *The Fontana Dictionary of Modern Thought* (London: Fontana).

Bullock, A. and Woodings, R. B. (eds) (1983). *The Fontana Biographical Companion to Modern Thought* (London: Fontana).

Buzan, T. (1974). *Use Your Head* (London: BBC).

Connolly, W. E. (1974). *The Terms of Political Discourse* (Lexington, Massachusetts: Heath).

Cross, C. (1983). *More Sayings of the Week From 'The Observer'* (Newton Abbott: David and Charles).

de Bono, E. (1970). *The Uses of Lateral Thinking* (Harmondsworth: Penguin).

de Bono, E. (1971). *The Mechanism of Mind* (Harmondsworth: Penguin).

Dunleavy, P. J. (1980). *Urban Political Analysis* (London: Macmillan).

Edelman, M. (1964). *The Symbolic Uses of Politics* (Urbana, Illinois: University of Illinois Press).

Galbraith, J. K. (1969). *The New Industrial State* (Harmondsworth: Penguin).

Gallie, W. B. (1956). 'Essentially contested concepts', *Proceedings of the Aristotelian Society*, vol. 56.

Gibbs, G. (1981). *Teaching Students How to Learn* (Milton Keynes: The Open University Press).

Goethe von, J. W. (1958). *Great Writings of Goethe* (New York: New American Library).

Habermas, J. (1973). *Knowledge and Human Interests* (London: Heinemann).

Hillery, G. A. (1955). 'Definitions of community', *Rural Sociology*, vol. 20, pp. 111–23.

International Encyclopaedia of the Social Sciences (1968). Edited by D. Sils (New York: Macmillan and Free Press), seventeen volumes.

Lewis, B. N. (1974). 'New methods of assessment and stronger methods of curriculum design' (Milton Keynes: Open University Institute for Educational Technology), unpublished report to the Ford Foundation.

Lindblom, C. E. (1959). 'The science of "muddling through"', *Public Administration Review*, vol. 19.

Lindblom, C. E. and Cohen, D. K. (1979), *Useable Knowledge: Social Science and Social Problem Solving* (New Haven: Yale University Press).

Lonergan, B. (1958). *Insight* (London: Ward Lock), reprinted 1978.

Macdonald-Ross, M. (1972). 'The problem of representing knowledge' (Paper to the Structural Learning Conference, Philadelphia).

Main, A. (1980). *Encouraging Effective Learning: An Approach to Study Counselling* (Edinburgh: Scottish Academic Press).

McLuan, M. (1959). 'Myth and mass media', *Daedalus*, vol. 88.

Mueller, D. C. (1979). *Public Choice* (Cambridge: Cambridge University Press).

Perry, W. G. (1970). *Forms of Intellectual and Ethical Development in the College Years* (New York: Holt, Rinehart and Winston).

Piaget, J. (1972). *Structuralism* (London: Routledge and Kegan Paul).

Rowntree, D. (1982). *Learn How to Study* (London: Macdonald).

Waller, R. (1977). 'Three functions of text presentation' (Milton Keynes: Open University Institute of Educational Technology), 'Notes on Transforming' series, no. 2.

Index